LOST
MIAMI

DAVID BULIT

LOST
MIAMI

STORIES AND SECRETS BEHIND MAGIC CITY RUINS

THE
History
PRESS

Published by The History Press
Charleston, SC 29403
www.historypress.net

All images are from the author's collection.

First published 2015

ISBN 978-1-5402-1338-9

Library of Congress Control Number: 2015943637

Notice: The information in this book is true and complete to the best of our knowledge. It is offered without guarantee on the part of the author or The History Press. The author and The History Press disclaim all liability in connection with the use of this book.

CONTENTS

ACKNOWLEDGEMENTS

My thanks go out to all the people who made this possible. My gratitude goes out to Zoo Miami, the largest and oldest zoo in Florida, for granting me permission to photograph the old military structures from the former Richmond Naval Air Station. Thanks to Jessica Klumb for giving us a personal tour around the Zoo Miami and Crandon Park properties and to Phil for sharing his firsthand memories. My gratitude also goes out to Arthur Lemaster for sharing his memories and information from his time working at the Aerojet facility.

A personal thank-you to my friends Dan and David for the explorations we've experienced together over the past years. I look forward to the years to come! Also, a special thanks to Xola for pushing me to move forward with this project and for inspiring me during our times together.

Finally, none of this would have been possible without Nomeus, who started Flurbex, a community for Florida's urban explorers where they can share with one another their work, experiences and ideas. Without Flurbex, my interests in urban exploring and photography probably wouldn't have grown into what they are today.

INTRODUCTION

In 1891, Julia Tuttle bought and lived in the area north of the Miami River where the city of Miami is now located. She decided to take a leading role in starting a new city but knew that decent transportation was paramount in attracting any type of development. In 1894, railroad magnate Henry Flagler built a railway from New York and ended it in Palm Beach, seeing little reason to extend it any farther south into what he considered a wilderness, despite Julia Tuttle's repeated offers to divide up the land she owned.

A great freeze occurred in 1985, wiping out orange groves throughout north and central Florida. It's not known why Flagler decided to extend his railroad farther, but legend has it that Tuttle sent him a bouquet of flowers and oranges from her citrus plantation in Miami to show that her grove had been spared.

The city of Miami grew rapidly due to the expansion of the railroad. By 1900, there were 1,681 people living in Miami; by 1910, there were 5,471, and by 1920, there were nearly 30,000 people. The city had grown so rapidly that visitors remarked that it had "grown like magic," and Miami came to be known as the "Magic City."

Almost a century later, Miami is still growing and expanding. Having lived here my whole life, I've seen what growth does and how some people will find every opportunity to erase history and replace it with multimillion-dollar condominiums. Though Miami is known for being a popular vacation destination, with beautiful beaches, a thriving nightlife and an abundance of different cultures, there are stories and history here that even people who live in the city probably don't know.

In this book, I try to bring to light places in and around Miami that have historical value but have been forgotten and left abandoned. Though many of the places I will be talking about have potential and can be preserved for future generations, you will find many more that are too far gone to have any chance at being saved.

PART I

THE TAMIAMI TRAIL

Construction of the Tamiami Trail's north–south section, which extends to Naples, began in 1915. Captain James Franklin Jaudon, who established and was involved in most of the road construction in Miami during the 1910s and 1920s, wanted to develop his holdings in the Everglades and proposed a road that connected Florida's Gulf and Atlantic Coasts. In Tampa, E.P. Dickey of the Board of Trade seconded the proposal and suggested the name the Tamiami Trail, "Tamiami" being a combination of Tampa and Miami.

At the time, Collier County did not yet exist, and the area was instead part of Lee County. In 1919, due to financial reasons, Lee County was not able to complete its portion of the Tamiami Trail. James Jaudon had already purchased 207,360 acres of land, mostly in Monroe County. He proposed changing the original route and redirecting it through Monroe County. With the use of his company, the Chevelier Corporation, he offered to build a link of the highway through his holdings in Monroe County. Dade and Lee Counties agreed to the proposal, and the Chevelier Corporation began laying out a new route for the road. In 1921, construction began on the new segment of the Tamiami Trail known today as Loop Road.

The State of Florida ran out of construction funds for the east–west portion in 1922. The following year, Barron Collier, an advertising mogul and entrepreneur who had recently diversified his holdings by investing in various types of businesses and millions of acres of southwest Florida wilderness, agreed to fund the completion of the Tamiami Trail in exchange for the establishment of a new county named after him.

Monroe Station, located on the Tamiami Trail near the entrance to Loop Road.

MOGUL, ENTREPRENEUR, BUSINESSMAN

Barron Gift Collier was born in Memphis, Tennessee, in 1873. His family was not poor, but Collier left school at the age of sixteen and began working for the railroad. Shortly thereafter, he made his first big business deal. Reading that the city of Memphis was interested in bringing gaslights to its streets, he convinced the city to give him exclusive rights on the streetlamps, and he was on his way to fame and fortune. With the proceeds, he purchased a printing company that had a contract to print signs for the horse-drawn streetcars in Memphis. Barron had read that electric streetcars were coming, and he once again secured the contract to print the advertising for the sides of the electric cars. He then branched out to other cities like Little Rock and New Orleans. Collier had made his first million by the age of twenty-six, and he moved his advertising business to New York in search of larger and more plentiful opportunities. By the time Barron Collier made his first visit to the Florida home of a friend on Useppa Island, he was earning an estimated $5 million a year.

Falling in love with the area around Charlotte Harbor, Collier set about acquiring land and beginning development. Eventually, he would own more than one million acres in what are now Lee, Hendry and Collier Counties. He would start the newspapers that would become the *Fort Myers News-Press* and the *Naples Daily News*. Collier West Coast Motor Lines is now known as Trailways. He also brought the first phone service to the area. In recognition of his contributions—and some say in exchange for his building the Tamiami Trail—part of Lee County was renamed to Collier County in 1923.

Perhaps his greatest accomplishment and legacy would be the construction of the Tamiami Trail, a road to link Tampa and Miami that was cut through the heart of the Everglades. With the goal of bringing services and new residents to the area, construction began in 1923, funded by Collier. Engineers, laborers, cooks and every sort of support personnel you can think of joined a traveling city that worked its way across the swamps, dredging, blasting and building as they went, sometimes making it only 150 feet in a day. Crews endured mosquitoes, snakes, alligators, oppressive heat and unending muck and saw grass. They were housed in large ox-drawn barracks that moved with the work. Construction was completed in 1928

with much fanfare and a motorcade cavalcade led by Collier from Tampa to Miami. Southwest Florida would no longer be isolated and inaccessible. The landscape and the small towns would never be the same.

The financial strain of the road's construction and the Great Depression combined to force Collier into filing bankruptcy, but the laws at the time allowed him to retain possession of all of his holdings. He died in 1939, just days shy of his sixty-sixth birthday.

While unpopular with many locals in his time, Barron Collier's impact and the continued influence of his family can be seen all over southwest Florida, from the county bearing his name to resorts, developments, financial institutions, roads, schools, libraries and museums, and the Tamiami Trail still serves to connect Miami to Florida's west coast. It stands as a marvel of construction in one of the most inhospitable environments in the world.

THIRTEEN YEARS TO COMPLETION

In 1923, Collier County was created out of the southern portion of Lee County, and almost immediately contention arose over the new deal. The original route of the Tamiami Trail ran completely through Collier County, and this was the route the State Road Department supported. The Board of County Commissioners of Dade County gave its support to the Chevelier Corporation since so much money had already been invested and only a few miles of the road were left before completion. Nonetheless, the State Road Department reinstated the original route, and the already completed portion of roadway in Monroe County became known as "South Loop."

Construction started on the east–west stretch in 1923. With the use of dynamite, a canal was created along the stretch of planned route, and the fill dirt was used to construct the roadway.

The Tamiami Trail took thirteen years, cost $8 million at the time and used 2.6 million sticks of dynamite in its construction. Considered a feat of engineering, the Tamiami Trail officially opened on April 25, 1928.

1

MONROE STATION

On the Tamiami Trail, halfway between Miami and Naples, sits a ramshackle and decrepit building known as Monroe Station. Monroe Station was one of six waystations established by Barron Collier in 1928 to service motorists traveling the newly constructed 107-mile section of the Tamiami Trail between Naples and Miami.

Operated by husband-and-wife teams, these stations were situated every ten miles along the portion of U.S. 441 that linked Naples and Miami, offering fuel, food and other necessities. Each station hosted a restaurant with a restroom on the ground floor and living quarters on the top floor for the husband and wife.

The stations also provided roadway security in the form of the Southwest Florida Mounted Police, created by David Graham Copeland. Appointed by the Collier County Sheriff's Office, the husbands would patrol a five-mile stretch on each side of their stations by motorcycle during daylight hours to assist motorists in need. These men became the foundation for the first Florida Highway Patrol.

In November 1928, Monroe Station was first operated by William Irwin; his wife, Nettie; and their two children. William Irwin died less than two months later, on January 19, 1929, in a head-on collision while on patrol on his motorcycle.

William J. Weaver was appointed as Irwin's replacement by the Collier County Sheriff's Office on January 26, 1929. His wife, Lillian, and their two daughters had moved into Monroe Station with him by the middle of February. The Weavers remained at Monroe Station until 1932. Lillian Weaver recalled that when she and her husband departed Monroe Station in 1932, a woman named Bertha and her daughter assisted them. She added, "Bertha then married Earl McGill, and they took over the station when we left." It is not known how long the McGills stayed at Monroe, but it's likely

they left when the Southwest Florida Mounted Police was disbanded in 1934.

Along with the collapse of the land boom in 1926 and the worldwide recession in 1929, the State Highway Department became responsible for enforcing laws on state roads in 1931, and the Division of Traffic Enforcement was created in 1934. These factors led to the eventual demise of the Southwest Florida Mounted Police.

In the 1930s, Barron G. Collier began experiencing financial problems that most likely had an impact on the Collier Corporation's Manhattan Mercantile Company, which managed the stores in the company town of Everglades City and the six service stations along the Tamiami Trail. These factors, along with the worsening economic conditions at the time, led to a reduction in travelers along the Tamiami Trail and, in turn, the closure and change in ownership of the Tamiami waystations.

Despite selling some of the stations, the Collier Corporation retained ownership of Monroe Station. It was suggested in a 1976 family history that Barron Collier never lost "complete faith in Florida's future as an investment and as a home place for millions of Americans."

The top floor of Monroe Station, where the owners lived.

MEMORIES OF MONROE STATION

Previous residents of Monroe Station recall memories of their time living out there during the 1940s. They spoke about living in Coral Gables, and they were only teenagers when their parents took over the waystation in 1945. They attended high school in Miami Monday through Friday and spent weekends at the station.

At the time, there was no electricity, so a generator was used to charge twelve-volt batteries to provide lighting, and gas was pumped by hand. The teens became friends with the neighboring Miccosukee Indians, who accompanied them on long walks down Loop Road to observe the wildlife in the area. When they swam in the canal that ran adjacent to the Tamiami Trail, the Miccosukee children would sit on the bank of the canal and yell out when they spotted an alligator nearby. The former residents also recalled that their mother would help produce aprons and pillowcases

The inside of Monroe Station, where the restaurant was located.

The kitchen area inside Monroe Station.

in traditional patchwork style for the native Miccosukee. During the 1947 hurricane, they boarded up the building and stayed at the Standard Oil Station in Ochopee, just down the road from them; it was a concrete building where everyone in the area gathered for safety against the rain and high winds.

Keith King moved into Monroe Station on September 1, 1960, along with his family, and stayed there until May 30, 1961, when he sold the station to Milton and Holly Arnold. The Arnolds lived there for just five months before selling it back to the King family in October 1961. The Kings lived at the station for a few years until they sold it again to Dixie Webb in the late 1960s.

Dixie Webb stayed at the station only from Friday to Sunday, but his manager, "Dynamite," stayed there full time from 1970 to 1972, before it was sold.

BIG CYPRESS ESTABLISHMENT AND TAKEOVER

In the early 1970s, Monroe Station was operated by "Big" Joe Lord and his wife, Susie. It was said that Big Joe was always angry, be it

P.S.
Even a Yankee would l...
Cookin'!

DADE CASH RE...
NATIONAL CASH REGISTER... Rebuil...
Clean & Oil, Overhauling, Rebuild...
Adding Machines, Typewriters & Check...
Used & Reconditioned Cash Registers for Sale
45th TER.
AVE.
BILL BRAMBLE

5825 Sunset Drive
Miami, Florida 33143
555-3366

Naples Daily New...

Serving Naples, Marco, Everglades, Immokalee, Golden Gate, Boni... Springs

28 PAGES   NAPLES, FLA., THURSDAY AFTERN... 1971   AP WIREPHOTOS, NEA PICTURE...

Landowners' Represe... ive Says
Taking Big Cypress Would Be Crime

Ellis ...a... director, of
...research for the East ...ier
County Land Owners ...
...anned the proposed feder...
...ernment's purchase of...
...ress... as a "crim...
...ed no p... to us.

...uam in a
...ittee
...sular Affairs,
...en., Henry M.
...ns be has been
Dr. Jack M. Wid-
...landowners' im-
...committee chair-
...about 35,000

...would be needed to travel these
...eral hundred square miles
... the trails and logging
...is in big-tired buggies which
... can ... at exact cost
...

"Instead of traveling through
swamps as you expected you
will travel high elevated pine,
palmetto and prairie land with a
great portion of the time seeing
some of the most fertile and
desirable land of this stat... You
can travel for many ...
without seeing a real low
cypress strand, which is actually a river be... in before
Lake Okeechob... ...yked by
the flowing fl... These
low strands a...
...ns ... tha...

Golden Lion Motel for $20,000
per acre.

"Other land near here is
selling for $17,000 per acre for
residential lots. Alligator Alley
frontage is selling for $10,000 for
1¼ acres. This land has the
same potential value as the
Gold Coast of Florida. An oil
company recently paid almost
$300,000 for an acre near Disney
World.

"If this choice high ...a..
land is taken from these 35,000
families of which about 5,000
are Cubans who have sought
refuge from Castro, property
owners of our nation will never
...ave any security. Let's protect
the ...ture for our children.
These Cubans have been made
to believe that Democracy will
protect their God given rights...
"This land developed with
...ter control can give water ...
...e thousands of ponds in the
park where hundreds d...
...illions of fish die every dry
... It is 37¼ miles between

"Crime is a threat to ...
existence. ...at greater ...
...against people th...
... this land where...
...anned and dreamed to li...
balance of their lives ...
choice climate and loca...
our nation?

"The good rock fill of th...
area will gross $40,000 o...
per acre yielding a pro...
$15,000 or more per acre...
oil wells t...in...ng ...
area are richly pro...
Actually this area could b...
the most desirable of Cour...
for millions of wonderfu...
to retire in. These great ...
of our nation deserve th...
...ood and man can p...
...them."

Monroe Station
→

at Vietnam War protestors, pot smokers or men with long hair. He was also very open about his hatred for the government, which was poised to purchase the Big Cypress swamp at the time and possibly put him out of business. Sure enough, in 1974, the Big Cypress National Preserve was established to ensure the preservation, conservation and protection of the natural scenic flora and fauna of the Big Cypress watershed. Soon after, the Lords were forced to remove the gas tanks at Monroe Station, which was a big hit to their profits.

Monroe Station would close in 1987 due to a loss of profits throughout the years. Big Cypress National Preserve later took over ownership of the station, boarding it up and ultimately neglecting it for years. It sat empty but was used in a movie called *Gone Fishin'*, released in 1997, starring Joe Pesci, Danny Glover, Rosanne Arquette and Willie Nelson.

Monroe Station was added to the National Register of Historic Places in 2000 without the knowledge of the National Park Service. The building was damaged in 2004 by Hurricane Wilma, requiring that a decision be made about the future of the historic property.

Only two of the original ten waystations remain today: Monroe Station and a gas station on the corner of Highway 92 and the Tamiami Trail. The Big Cypress National Park Service has turned the backside of Monroe Station into a rest stop and camping area and is looking at options for the best way to renovate the building.

Opposite, top: An old newspaper clipping about the National Park Service's takeover of the Big Cypress Preserve.

Opposite, bottom: A sign on the side of the Tamiami Trail indicating where Monroe Station is located.

2

WILLIAM ANDERSON GENERAL MERCHANDISE STORE

The years between 1910 and 1920 saw Dade County's population quadruple in size. The landscape was quickly evolving from deserted wetland swamps to rows of fields as rudimentary roads and auspicious homesteaders found their way south. Draining the lowlands provided ample opportunities for agricultural endeavors, and it was not long before extensive development was underway.

Because transportation between disparate settlements throughout the county was difficult, general stores provided a level of convenience to residents in outlying areas, including many farmers. Anderson's Corner is the last of these pioneer-era commercial properties still standing in Miami-Dade County.

William "Popp" Anderson came from Indiana in the early days of the twentieth century to join his friend and hunting companion Charles Grossman, the first settler in the area. Silver Palm was known for its extensive pinelands and plentiful game. Anderson soon established a homestead just east of his friend's and just south of the Perrine land grant.

For some time, Anderson operated a commissary car for the Drake Lumber Company, providing staples and necessities for workers in remote lumber camps. In 1911, he established the William Anderson General Merchandise Store, which sold myriad items to residents and businesses. With living quarters on the second floor, Anderson's Corner was strategically located across from the Silver Palm School at the intersection of two well-built roads. It sold a large selection of items to the nearby residents and businesses; the only other option to purchase items was the town of Cutler Bay, some fifteen miles away.

After serving as a general store until the 1930s, it was converted into apartments. Finally condemned in 1975, a reprieve was granted for rehabilitation. Listed on the National

The kitchen area at Anderson's Corner.

Opposite, top: William Anderson's General Store, aka Anderson's Corner.

Opposite, bottom: The top floor of Anderson's Corner.

Register of Historic Places in 1977, the site became a local historic location in October 1981, and rehabilitation of the structure was completed in 1985. Sometime later, it became the Harvest House restaurant and was highly praised among the farming community in the area.

The building was heavily damaged in 1992, when Hurricane Andrew made landfall in Homestead as a Category 5 hurricane. That storm has had a long-lasting effect on parts of South Florida.

There have been renovation efforts over the years, but none has been successful. Though the exterior of the building looks to be in decent shape, the interior has been gutted to the point where there are no walls or a floor on the bottom level. Navigating the floor is possible only by walking on slabs of plywood that have been laid across the wooden beams.

Today, a small cafeteria and convenience store calling themselves Anderson's Corner operate adjacent

The ground floor of Anderson's Corner.

to the old Anderson's Corner. The only people who seem to take interest in the building are a couple who feed the stray cat population and a farmer who keeps chickens on the property.

PART II

SECRETS OF THE MAGIC CITY

In May 1960, Fidel Castro established diplomatic relations with the Soviet Union. This led to the United States blocking all imports from Cuba and severing any diplomatic relations it had with that country. With approval from President Dwight D. Eisenhower, the Central Intelligence Agency (CIA) began recruiting Cuban exiles in the Miami area to equip and train them for an invasion of the island. This group of 1,400 paramilitary and contract soldiers would be known as Brigade 2506.

In January 1961, the United States pushed its plans for an invasion into motion despite advisors to the new president, John. F. Kennedy, maintaining that Cuba posed no real threat to America. Kennedy had his own doubts about the plan as well, thinking the Soviets would see the invasion as an act of war and retaliate,

but CIA officers stressed that they would keep U.S. involvement in the invasion a secret.

On April 15, 1961, a group of Cuban exiles took off from Nicaragua for Cuba in a squadron of American B-26 bombers, painted with the false flag markings of the Fuerza Aérea Revolucionaria (FAR), the air force of the Cuban government, and began bombarding Cuban airfields to destroy Castro's small air force. However, Castro and his advisors had known of the impending raid and moved the planes out of harm's way. The plan was too far along to stop, and on April 17, 1961, Brigade 2506 landed at an isolated spot on the island's southern shore known as the Bay of Pigs.

The invasion was a disaster from the beginning. Many exiles drowned as coral reefs sank their ships when they pulled into shore. Paratroopers landed in the wrong places, and it didn't take long for Cuban forces to corner them on the beach, killing 114 and capturing over 1,100 of the exiles.

In response to the failed Bay of Pigs invasion, Castro reached out to the Soviets for help against any further threats of aggression by the United States. The Soviets agreed to his request and deployed a number of nuclear missiles in Cuba to prevent any future harassment. This event would later be known as the Cuban Missile Crisis.

After months of tense negotiations between the United States and the USSR, the Soviets agreed to dismantle the nuclear weapons; in exchange, the United States made a public declaration and agreement to never invade Cuba without direct provocation. CIA operations would continue in and around the Miami area throughout the years as the Cold War dragged on for another three decades.

3

RICHMOND NAVAL AIR STATION

Lieutenant Nelson Grills and his crew of nine departed the Richmond Naval Air Station aboard a K-74, along with another airship, to provide escort for a freighter and a tanker that would be passing through the Straits of Florida. Grills's orders were to pilot his airship to a position in the upper keys, while the other aircraft would take a longer, more southerly course. With the ever-present threat of German U-boats, the crew was alert to the danger. Shortly before midnight on July 18, 1943, the K-74's radar picked up the two ships it was to oversee and then a third unidentified blip. The K-74 moved to investigate the unknown intruder.

In the warm night air, *U-134* was running on the surface recharging its batteries as it closed in on the two merchant ships. Without time to wait for help from surface ships or fighter planes, Grills ordered his blimp to attack the submarine in an attempt to draw fire from the sub and save the vessels he was sent to protect. Fire from the deck gun of the U-boat ripped into the air, enveloping one of the blimp's engines and igniting a fire, while the crew of the K-74 fired back and dropped depth charges. In a few very short minutes, it was over. The stricken airship settled into the water as *U-134* slipped away.

The crew of the airship all survived the shelling, fire and crash; unfortunately, one crewman, Isadora Stessel, became separated from the group and was killed by sharks. Grills faced intense scrutiny for his decision to attack without waiting for support, but it was determined that his actions probably saved one, if not both, of the merchant vessels. The entire crew was awarded Purple Hearts. It was not until 1961, when records from the Kriegsmarine were reviewed, that it was discovered that the actions of the K-74 had damaged *U-134* and prevented it from diving, allowing it to later be sunk. In light of this new information, Grills was

A ghost sign reading, "NAS Richmond" at the Gold Coast Railroad Museum.

awarded the Distinguished Flying Cross. The K-74 was the only airship lost to enemy fire during the war.

After the Japanese attack on Pearl Harbor and the United States' entrance into World War II, Adolf Hitler ordered his U-boats to move closer to the United States in order to attack ships traveling along the coast. Since the onset of the war, German U-boats had been wreaking havoc on Allied shipping throughout the Atlantic, but now ships were being torpedoed and left burning within sight of American coastal cities. With the U.S. Navy and Coast Guard's surface ships stretched thin providing escorts to transatlantic convoys, blimps came into service for antisubmarine uses. Construction of bases began in early 1942.

One such base was Richmond Naval Air Station (NAS), just west of Miami. In 1941, the navy purchased 2,100 acres around the sawmill community of Richmond (where the base would get its name) and began what would be the largest construction project ever undertaken in Dade County up to that time. When completed, there would be a two-thousand-foot-diameter landing pad, eight support pads, two runways, a helium plant, three enormous hangars, twenty-five airships and three thousand men stationed at Richmond NAS.

The construction of the hangars would be a nearly overwhelming undertaking. Work on each hangar was begun by building huge 148-foot-tall concrete door supports for each corner. These unique pillars would hold the massive steel doors and support the rest of the structure. Once completed, each hangar would be more than 1,086 feet long and

183 feet high and enclose a full seven acres. Combined, the three hangars would be able to accommodate the twenty-five airships assigned to the air station, along with airplanes, automobiles, machine shops, storage and parts and equipment to keep the blimps on patrol.

Richmond NAS was officially commissioned on September 15, 1942, and the impact on the war effort was quickly felt. With the blimps from Richmond, combined with the improvement to the Civil Air Patrol and the use of convoys for coastal freighters, successful torpedo attacks near Florida fell from 114 in 1942 to just 4 in 1943. In a stretch from November 1943 through May 1945, airships from Richmond NAS logged 730 days on continuous patrol without the loss of a single ship.

As it turned out, the greatest threat to the air station would not come at the hands of an enemy nation but from Mother Nature. In September 1945, a hurricane raced across the Atlantic headed for the Florida coast.

A bomb shelter located at the Zoo Miami grounds.

In preparation for the impending threat, air bases from the area and the aircraft carrier USS *Guadalcanal* sent their planes to Richmond to be kept safe inside the massive, heavily built hangars.

1945 HOMESTEAD HURRICANE

On September 15, 1945, three years to the day after the base was commissioned, a large hurricane came ashore and made a direct strike on the hangars and buildings of the Richmond NAS. Winds over 125 miles per hour hammered the base, causing minor damage, but during the storm a fire broke out in one of the hangars. Driven by the hurricane-force wind and fueled by paints, aircraft fuel, oil and the nearly two million board feet of Douglas fir in each hangar, the fire quickly spread to all three. By the time the storm passed, the massive buildings had been reduced to ash and rubble. The only things left standing were the steel doors and the twelve concrete supports. Gone, too, were the more than 350 aircrafts, including Hellcats, Corsairs and P-51 Mustangs, along with 150 vehicles that had been brought inside to protect them from the storm.

With the war over and the German U-boat threat gone, the hangars would never be rebuilt. The base would continue its military life for several years as the navy used the helium plant to refuel blimps, but the property's importance to the area and the country would carry on for much longer.

In 1946, with soldiers returning home and enrollments up, 1,571 acres were deeded to the University of Miami for the creation of the South Campus. It would be used to house students and create laboratories and research facilities, many of which are still in use today.

The Gold Coast Railroad Museum began using part of the base's railroad tracks in 1956 and moved to the location of Hangars #1 and #2 in 1984. In addition to its extensive railroad history, the museum also has a collection of photos and memorabilia for Richmond NAS.

Richmond Air Force Station was constructed northwest of the blimp field in 1962. A radar facility, it housed three radar towers and remained in use until 1992, when another hurricane, Andrew, damaged the buildings and towers.

Opposite, top: An old boiler building at the former Richmond NAS blimp base.

Opposite, bottom: A train at the Gold Coast Railroad Museum.

JMWAVE

In 1961, the CIA moved into Building 25 on the South Campus of the University of Miami, using it as a listening post. Codenamed JMWAVE, Building 25 was established as the operations center for Operation Mongoose, a covert action to overthrow the Communist powers in Cuba that included the use of U.S. Special Forces, the destruction of Cuban sugar crops and mining the waters around harbors.

JMWAVE reached its peak in late 1962, during the Cuban Missile Crisis. Between 1962 and 1965, JMWAVE grew to be the largest CIA station in the world, other than its headquarters in Virginia. The station had an estimated three to four hundred professional operatives, as well as over fifteen thousand anti-Cuban exiles who were trained in commando tactics and espionage and were supported by the station in numerous raids against Cuba.

The CIA became Miami's largest employer during this period. In addition to its main front company, Zenith Technical Enterprises Inc., the CIA created about three to four hundred other front companies throughout South Florida, as well as a large number of safe houses,

A small sign that reads, "US Property. No Trespassing."

cover businesses and other properties. JMWAVE's activities were so widespread that they became an open secret among local Florida government officials and law enforcement.

On June 26, 1964, *Look* magazine published an article exposing Zenith Technical Enterprises as a front for the CIA. By 1968, JMWAVE had been deemed obsolete, and out of concern that any public awareness of the CIA's activities would become an embarrassment for the University of Miami, the station was deactivated.

PRESENT USE AND LEGACY

In the 1970s, Miami-Dade County was deeded part of the former base's property for the construction of a new, larger zoo to replace the Crandon Park Zoo on Key Biscayne. Construction began in 1975, and the first exhibits were opened in 1980 as the Miami Metro Zoo. The parking lot for the zoo now occupies the two-thousand-foot-diameter main landing pad.

Recently, the Richmond Administration Building, the last remaining structure from the base, was moved from its original location in the government-owned area to a site near the zoo and railroad museum. The outside of the building has been restored, and work is underway on the interior. When complete, it will house the South Florida Military Museum.

An attempt was made to remove the twelve concrete door supports by using dynamite. Eleven of them fell, but one did not. Radio antennas were placed on top, and it still stands today, serving as a relay station for the area 911 system. It remains one of the tallest structures in the county.

Richmond NAS is now home to two museums, a zoo, a university, a U.S. Coast Guard installation and other government facilities. When seen from the air, the footprint of the air station is still very visible. The pads, runways and old hangar sites are clearly defined. However, the impact of Richmond NAS is not limited to the landscape or the war record of the base. It is also felt in the cultural and educational contributions to the community that are being made from the old blimp base.

Opposite: Inside a boiler building on the grounds of the former Richmond NAS blimp base.

4

NIKE MISSILE IFC SITE HM-95

In 1944, the United States Department of War demanded a new air defense system to combat the new jet aircraft, as existing gun-based systems proved largely incapable of dealing with the speeds and altitudes at which jet aircrafts operated. Two proposals were accepted. Bell Laboratories, a subsidiary of AT&T, proposed Project Nike, while a much longer-range collision-course system named Project Thumper was developed by General Electric.

Project Nike was developed to deal with bombers flying at five hundred miles per hour and at altitudes up to sixty thousand feet. At these speeds and heights, rockets and missiles were no longer fast enough to be simply aimed at a target. The missile would have to be "led" toward the target to ensure that the target was hit before it ran out of fuel. After much research, Bell scientists concluded:

A supersonic rocket missile should be vertically launched under the thrust of a solid-fuel booster which was then to be dropped; thence, self-propelled by a liquid-fuel motor, the missile should be guided to a predicted intercept point in space and detonated by remote control commands; these commands should be transmitted by radio signals determined by a ground-based computer associated with radar which would track both the target and the missile in flight.

The Nike system utilized three radars: the Acquisition Radar searched for a target to be handed over to the Target Tracking Radar for tracking, and the Missile Tracking Radar (MTR) tracked the missile by way of a transponder, as the missile's radar signature alone was not sufficient. The MTR also commanded

the missile by way of pulse-position modulation. The pulses were received, decoded and then amplified back for the MTR to track. Once the tracking radars were locked, the system was able to work automatically following launch, barring any unexpected occurrences. The computer then compared the two radars' directions, along with information on the speeds and distances, to calculate the intercept point and steer the missile toward the target.

In March 1948, the Key West Agreement was reached; it stated the functions of the United States Army, Navy and newly created Air Force, which was a major step toward delineating the differences in their roles and missions. A prominent feature was an outline of the division of air assets that continue to be the basis of the U.S. military today. According to the agreement, the navy would be allowed to retain its own combat air assets. The army was allowed to retain aviation assets for the purpose of recon and medical evacuation. The air force would gain control of all strategic air assets, as well as most logistical and tactical functions.

Due to this, the air force took control of all long-range systems and merged them with Project Thumper, while the army continued to work on Project Nike. In 1950, the army formed the Army Anti-Aircraft Command (ARAACOM), which was in charge of operating antiaircraft gun and missile batteries. ARAACOM would

The main entrance to the barracks at the Nike Missile IFC HM-95 site.

later be renamed the U.S. Army Air Defense Command (USARADCOM), shortened to ARADCOM in 1961.

NIKE AJAX

The first successful Nike missile test occurred in November 1951, intercepting a drone B-17 flying fortress. Nike Ajax (MIM-3) were the first type of missiles built and were deployed starting in 1953. The missiles were able to reach a maximum of one thousand miles per hour and an altitude of seventy thousand feet and had a range of just twenty-five miles. The missiles' limited range was seen as a serious flaw, which meant they had to be deployed close to the area they were protecting, so they were positioned strategically to protect key points of interest such as cities and military installations. By 1962, over 240 launch sites had been built, replacing the National Guard and army's antiaircraft gun emplacements.

The Nike batteries were set up in what were known as defense areas surrounding cities and at strategic locations such as nuclear power plants and ICBM sites. The Nike sites were numbered from one to ninety-nine and increased clockwise, so Nike sites numbered between one and twenty-five were usually in the northeast, twenty-six to fifty were in the southeast, fifty-one to seventy-five were in the southwest and seventy-six to ninety-nine were in the northwest. They were also preceded by a one- or two-letter code that related to the city they were protecting. For example, situated in Key Largo, HM-40 meant that it was part of the Homestead AFB/Miami Defense Area and that it could be found southeast of the Homestead and Miami areas.

In response to the Cuban Missile Crisis, involving the deployment of Russian nuclear missiles in Cuba, on October 25, 1962, the Second Missile Battalion of the Fifty-second Air Defense Artillery was deployed in South Florida under the command of the Thirteenth Air Artillery Group. Forming a circle around Miami and Homestead, its mission was to defend against the threat of bombers and fighters. Meant to be a temporary solution, the South Florida units lived in tent cities in the Everglades swamps, cow pastures and farmland.

In April 1963, the South Florida missile sites became a permanent part of ARADCOM, and in August 1963, the army announced that the South Florida missile sites would become a permanent feature in the United States' air defense network. In 1965, the batteries relocated

Opposite: Looking down a hallway at the Nike Missile IFC HM-95 site.

to newly constructed sites and were granted certification in the use of nuclear warheads for their missiles.

THE SITE

Named after Homestead AFB/ Miami Defense Area, HM-95 was activated in October 1962 on Krome Avenue, just south of the Tamiami Trail and west of downtown Miami. Like most other Nike sites, it was built in three parts. One part was the Launcher area, which held up to three underground missile magazines, each serving a group of four launch assemblies. The Launcher area was located where the Krome Immigration Detention Center is today. Another part contained the Integrated Fire Control (IFC) radar systems, a group of three radars used to detect incoming targets and to direct the missiles, along with the computer system, to plot and direct the intercept. The last part was the Administration, which was usually built alongside the Integrated Fire Control site. This part included the battery headquarters, barracks, mess, recreation hall and motor pool.

Inside the barracks at the Nike Missile IFC HM-95 site.

As the Nike Ajax was being tested, work had already begun on the Nike Hercules missile (MIM-14), a much more powerful missile with greater range and more destructive force than the older Ajax missiles. It had improved speed, topping three thousand miles per hour; improved range capable of up to one hundred miles; and a maximum altitude of 100,000 feet. The missile also had the option to be equipped with a nuclear warhead, guaranteeing a kill. By 1963, the Homestead AFB/Miami Defense Area sites, including HM-95, had been equipped with Hercules missiles.

PHASING OUT OF ARADCOM

By the end of the 1960s, the Vietnam War had an indirect influence on ARADCOM. With the mounting cost of operations in Vietnam and growing inflation in the United States, ARADCOM was partially dismantled. During the early 1970s, the "Vietnamization" program was developed, which involved expanding, equipping and training South Vietnam forces while steadily reducing the number of U.S.

The courtyard area at the Nike Missile IFC HM-95 site.

combat troops there. Once most of the U.S. troops were pulled out of Vietnam, the United States began to reduce the size of its military.

Going into the '70s, the Soviets had modernized and increased their strategic ballistic missiles, opting for more land-based and submarine-launched ballistic missile than bomber aircrafts. By the end of 1971, the Soviet Union had an estimated 1,424 ICBM launchers in service at ICBM complexes, 90 percent of them believed to be inside of protective silos. In 1973, a change in the United States' air defense policy was made, as it was stated that it was beyond the nation's technological capabilities to protect populated areas from a coordinated nuclear strike.

Many of the Nike sites in the United States were decommissioned, and by May 1974, ARADCOM's operational air defense force consisted of four Nike Hercules batteries and four Nike Hawk batteries in the Homestead AFB/Miami Defense Area and four Nike Hawk batteries in the Key West Defense Area. In October 1974, ARADCOM was disbanded, and control of the South Florida sites was transferred to the U.S. Army Forces Command (FORSCOMM).

Despite the disbandment of ARADCOM, the South Florida sites remained operational due to their proximity to nearby communist countries. In 1975, the joint chiefs of staff ordered the army to remove all W-31 nuclear warheads and replace them with T-45 conventional high explosives. In 1979, the South Florida Nike missile batteries, which included HM-03, HM-40, HM-66, HM69 and HM-95, were decommissioned.

FROM REFUGEE CAMP TO GHOST STORY

In 1980, the Administration and IFC areas were used as a refugee camp to temporarily house Cuban refugees during the Mariel boatlift. The Mariel boatlift was a large immigration of Cubans to the United States, including a number who were released from Cuban prisons and mental institutions. The Launcher area was used as a detention center for those who were considered dangerous and high risk or who suffered from mental disorders and needed to be segregated. A year later, in May 1981, the camp was converted into a permanent federal detention center for Cuban, Haitian and other non-Americans deemed criminals, deportees or mentally unstable. Today, the detention center is known as the Krome Service Processing Center.

In 1985, the IFC site was reused as a CIA Office of Communications Regional Relay Facility high-frequency radio transmitter site. The high-frequency receiver site and a larger agency facility were located on the grounds of the former Richmond

The generator building at the Nike Missile IFC HM-95 site.

Opposite: Looking down a hallway at the Nike Missile IFC HM-95 site.

Naval Air Station. Both sites had signs indicating they were U.S. Army Regional Communications Activity stations. In conjunction with another CIA operation at the Richmond Naval Air Station, they relayed messages to operatives in the Caribbean and South America. The IFC site also housed a mobile command center that would be used in case of a nuclear crisis. In 1992, due to damages caused by Hurricane Andrew, the facility was abandoned.

Abandoned and neglected, the IFC site became known by many as a "penit," a term used when describing any building or set of buildings used for the purpose of illegal graffiti and frequented by a variety of taggers. The site is also a popular place for paintball wars and weekend bonfires.

Due to its history of housing mentally ill refugees, it has become local urban legend that it was a secret mental asylum where ghosts and murderers still reside. Some people claim to have seen a woman in a white gown, a past resident of the asylum, strolling the compound and asking for help. Others have said they've been chased out by a man in a black bandana wielding a

machete, allegedly a father who took his newborn child to the abandoned building and butchered him inside. A few even claim that the property was actually a secret detention center where they used to house Korean spies, but you won't find that information anywhere because it's something "the government doesn't want you to know about." However, the truth is much more interesting.

5

AEROJET-DADE ROCKET MANUFACTURING PLANT AND TEST SITE

In 1957, Sputnik was launched, becoming the first human-made object to orbit the Earth—an event that sparked two space races, one between the United States and the Soviet Union and the other between the United States Air Force and the newly created National Aeronautics and Space Administration (NASA). In 1963, the U.S. Air Force gave Aerojet General, a major rocket and missile propulsion manufacturer, $3 million to start construction of a manufacturing and testing site in Homestead, no more than five miles from the entrance to the Everglades National Park.

A small debate arose about whether to use liquid-fuel rocket engines, solid-fuel rocket motors or a combination of the two. The rocket would need massive thrust capabilities, enough to lift 100,000 pounds of payload to space, which favored solid fuel. But once free of the Earth's orbit, liquid fuel seemed to be the best route, as the crafts could then be steered. Early on, NASA's Wernher Von Braun favored a liquid-fueled rocket, which would later be used in the Saturn V project.

Aerojet's main competitor was Thiokol, which built segmented solid motors that were manufactured in segments and then transported by rail to the site to be assembled there. Aerojet preferred the monolithic approach, which meant the motor was built in one piece. This was a much safer approach, as any problems with the joints of a segmented motor could lead to disaster.

THE FACILITY

Among potential sites such as Daytona Beach, California and Texas, Homestead was chosen as the place where Aerojet's new facility would be built. Aerojet acquired land for its new facility, paying $2.50 an acre

per year for an annual lease, with an option to buy up to twenty-five thousand acres more at nickels on the dollar.

A proposal was approved to dig a canal from the facility's location to Barnes Sound, south of Biscayne Bay. This would allow barges to carry the giant rocket motors between Cape Canaveral and the Homestead site via the canal and Intracoastal Waterway. Despite the fact that the Everglades National Park was less than five miles up the road from the facility, which opened in 1947, any potential environmental issues that could occur due to the digging of the canal were downplayed in favor of economic development. After the U.S. Senate bypassed environmental considerations, the C-111 canal was dug.

Aerojet now needed a cylindrical chamber that would withstand the force and power a space-traveling rocket would encounter. After much researching, it decided to subcontract the fabrication of 260-inch-diameter, 24-meter-long chambers to Sun Ship and Dry Dock Company located in Chester, Pennsylvania. The chambers were designed in short length, meaning half the size of what the final product would be, hence the name given to the test rockets: SL-1, SL-2 and SL-3. The motors used a propellant burning rate and nozzle size appropriate for the full-length design and were capable of an estimated three million pounds of thrust for 114 seconds.

Two rocket chambers were delivered to the facility, the first one in March 1965. At the time, the C-111 canal was not yet completed, so the rocket chamber was barged down from Sun Ship to Homestead via the Intracoastal Waterway and then trucked in from Biscayne Bay. The chamber was designated SL-1.

Once the chamber arrived at the site, it was lined with primer and insulation at the General Processing Building. This process was necessary, as it confined the massive pressure and intense heat that would occur during the test firings, as well as allowing an even curing of the propellant. Once completed, the chamber was then trucked three additional miles south of the complex to the Cast and Cure Center, where it would be filled with the propellant.

Meanwhile, the propellant was being prepared at the Oxidizer Preparation and Fuel Preparation Buildings, both of which were supervised by the Quality Control Lab. The components were then taken to the vertical batch and continuous batch mixers to be combined. Exact

Opposite, top: This building was used to construct and house the rocket motor at the Aerojet facility.

Opposite, bottom: Stripped machinery inside the Quality Control Lab at the Aerojet facility.

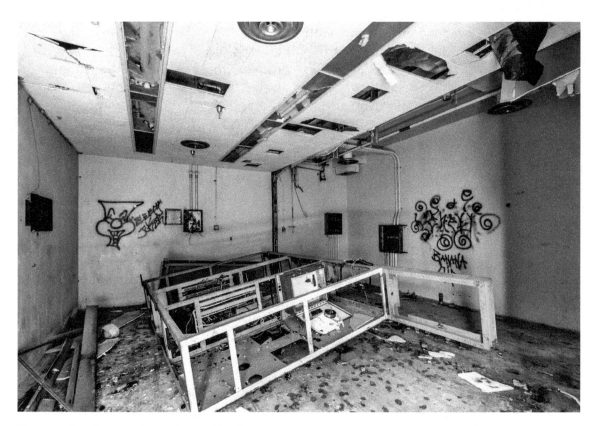

The remains of computer equipment inside one of the Fuel Preparation Buildings at the Aerojet facility.

measurements of fuel and oxidizer were mixed together and poured into large metal cylinders. Samples were then taken to the lab to verify that the components were combined accurately. Afterward, the propellant was stored in protective drums until casting.

At the center of the Cast and Cure Center was the test firing pit and test stand, a two-story shed that could be moved over the rocket motor during the casting and curing process and then moved out of the way during the actual test firing. About half a mile to the west was the blockhouse, which resembled a bunker. This was where the switch was flipped to begin the test firing.

THE TESTS

In May 1965, the Sl-1 was trucked down to the Cast and Cure Center, and it took workers over fourteen hours to lower it into the firing pit. Once the shed was put into place over the pit, trucks rolled out from the facility carrying the propellant with which the rocket motor would be filled. An intricate system of pumps and vacuums was used to fill the motor from the bottom up to ensure there were no air pockets present. Once started, the process had to be continuous, and workers worked nonstop, rotating through eight-hour shifts three times a day. It took three months to complete this process. After the filling process, the fuel was heat cured at 135 degrees Fahrenheit for three weeks followed by an additional two weeks for the fuel to cool. Once hardened, the solid fuel had a rubbery consistency, similar to that of a pencil eraser.

Afterward, a temporary platform was built for the next steps. The motor was capped, and a nozzle was put into place. The motor was then armed with an igniter, or a small rocket in this case.

On September 25, 1965, SL-1 was fired. The blast sent the igniter into the air to be guided by cables to a pond just east of the firing pit. Below the rocket motor, measurements were taken by the thrust rings and load cells while the blockhouse recorded further information during the test. After the test, a crane poured a mixture of water and carbon dioxide into the motor to stop the burning.

Having produced more than 3.3 million pounds of thrust, the test was a success, surpassing many expectations. After scheduling another test for the following year, Aerojet hosted a picnic for the workers and community to celebrate.

The SL-2 chamber arrived at the Aerojet facility weeks before the first test. Delivered by barge, it arrived with Hurricane Betsy in the vicinity. The barge was tied to a dock but was torn loose, causing both the barge and motor to become beached against the seawall. The chamber was undamaged, and with a bit of effort, the barge was put back in the water.

On February 23, 1966, SL-2 was successfully tested, burning for over two minutes and producing over 3.9 million pounds of thrust. Having been fired at night, the light from the flame was seen from as far as downtown Miami, some fifty kilometers away. The blast was heard as far as Islamorada, twenty-seven miles away, and reports came from Key West of a glowing light coming off the horizon. Though they were the same size, SL-2's thrust surpassed that of SL-1. Rather than landing in the pond, the ignitor was hurled out into the Everglades, where workers were later sent out to retrieve it.

With SL-2 deemed another success, plans for SL-3 were already underway when NASA requested $3.5 million for the next test. This time around, scientists wanted to test some new ideas to try to get even more power out of the rocket motor. The ideas consisted of modifying the rocket in three areas. A faster-burning propellant and wider exhaust nozzle

The Ford car garage at the Aerojet facility.

would produce more than five million pounds of thrust. The nozzle would be slightly submerged into the motor, and the control system would be put into place for a more consistent burn. It took sixteen months to implement all the modifications for the next test.

SL-3 was fired on June 17, 1967, producing over six million pounds of thrust, making it the largest solid-fueled rocket in history. During the test, chunks of propellant were ejected, causing the exit cone to shake loose and fly into the air. Farmers reported fall-out damage that caused black spots on their crops and grove trees. Paint and chrome on nearby cars were also corroded. As this test was much more powerful than the previous two, local residents voiced their concerns, stating that if the blast from a small rocket motor could shake windows, testing a full-scale rocket would surely shatter them. Aerojet told farmers and car owners to file claims and it would do all it could to ensure compensation for the damages if they were, in fact, caused by the firing. There were so many claims, however, that many were denied, prompting numerous lawsuits. It was later found that droplets of hydrochloric acid, a byproduct of the firing, were to blame for the damages.

END OF AN ERA

By 1969, NASA had decided to go with liquid-fueled engines for the *Apollo's* Saturn V rockets. A fourth chamber was built by Aerojet Azusa using a fiberglass casing, but it was never even hydro tested before funding was cut off, leaving many of the workers at the Florida facility without jobs. Aerojet essentially mothballed the facility, waiting to see if the U.S. government would change its mind. After the space shuttle *Challenger* and Titan34D disasters, both of which were victims of a solid rocket motor malfunction, Aerojet felt NASA and the U.S. Air Force would turn to safer monolithic designs.

In 1986, after NASA had awarded the space shuttle booster contract to Morton Thiokol, Aerojet sued the State of Florida and decided to pull out of South Florida for good. It sold most of its landholdings to the South Dade Land Corporation for $6 million, and after many unsuccessful attempts to use the land for farming, the acreage was sold off to the State of Florida for $12 million. Years later, Aerojet would trade its remaining 5,100 acres in South Florida for 55,000 acres of environmentally sensitive land belonging to the U.S. Bureau of Land Management in New Mexico.

During the Cold War, the CIA operated extensively throughout the South Florida area, owning many businesses and using them as fronts or safe houses. Operating out of the nearby Homestead Air Force Base, the CIA used the Aerojet facility for government training purposes. It's front was a carpet manufacturer running out of the Fuel Preparation Building, and anyone asking about the gunshots heard out there was told they were part of a police training exercise. In 1992, Hurricane Andrew would stop any further government training on the property, leading to its abandonment.

On May 11, 1996, ValuJet Flight 592 took off from Miami International Airport for Atlanta, Georgia, on a regularly scheduled trip. Shortly after takeoff, a fire occurred in the cargo compartment due to improperly stored oxygen generators, causing the plane to crash into the Everglades a few miles west of Miami. The plane was destroyed on impact, killing all 110 people on board. Due to the sheer amount of force, immersion in the swampy water and scavenging wildlife, only 68 bodies out of the 110 who died were identified, some by examining only a jawbone or, in one case, a torn piece of flesh.

On the third anniversary of the accident, a memorial was built eleven miles west of Krome Avenue, just north of the Tamiami Trail. Designed by students from the American Institute of Architecture and built by local masons and contractors at no cost, the memorial consists of 110 concrete pillars and points toward the location of the crash site some

eight miles north. A plaque can be found there with the names of all 110 victims. At some point, victim records and debris from the plane crash, including chairs and metal paneling, were stored at the Aerojet facility, inside the building where the fuel was tested. Years later, the interior of the building that held the ValuJet records was set on fire, destroying everything inside. It's presumed that any machinery and plane crash debris stored there was taken away, either as scrap metal or trash.

After the facility's complete abandonment, it became a popular hangout for vandals and scrappers. Signs erected along the road leading to the facility read, "Discharge of firearms is prohibited." Despite that, the area is littered with spent shotgun shells and bullet casings, and many of the signs along the road have bullet holes in them, including the ones prohibiting the use of firearms.

On Wednesday, September 4, 2013, eighteen-year-old Jesús Trejo was reported missing after his car was found on Southwest 232nd Avenue in Homestead, better known as Aerojet Road, which led to the abandoned rocket manufacturing facility.

After searching the surrounding area for several hours, police divers found his body not too far from where they found his car, in the canal that runs parallel to the road. Several news outlets reported a possible gunshot wound to the head and that there were signs that alligators had

The laboratory at the Aerojet facility.

Files and various other things, such as plane debris from the Valujet Flight 592 plane crash, were stored here at the Aerojet facility.

Opposite, top: Looking down the hallway of the Quality Assurance building at the Aerojet facility.

Opposite, bottom: Inside the Continuous Mixing Building at the Aerojet facility.

attacked him in the water.

Police have classified the case as a homicide, and it is still unknown who killed him and dumped his body in the canal. According to his aunt, all that is known is that he was going to meet some "white boy" in the Everglades. No one knows whom he went to meet out there or why. At the site where his body was found, surrounded by broken police caution tape and sun-dried flowers, remains a small memorial to Jesús Trejo, a reminder of how dangerous life can be.

ECOSYSTEM RESTORATION

The property and land surrounding the old Aerojet facility are now controlled by the South Florida Water Management District (SFWMD) and the Florida Fish and Wildlife Conservation Commission as a nature preserve. In February 2010, Rodney Erwin, representing the Omega Space Systems Group, made a

proposal to the Homestead City Council to resurrect the vacant Aerojet facility as a new rocket plant. Though Homestead mayor Steve Bateman supported the plan, pushing the need for jobs, the water management district immediately shot down the idea.

Since it was dug, the canal had been diverting a large volume of fresh water from most coastal wetlands and depositing this water into northeastern Florida Bay. Because of this, it had left parts of the bay too salty, making it a poor environment for fish, crabs and wading birds. The peat soil in Taylor Slough, a critical foundation for the Everglades, had also dried out and occasionally caught fire. Submerged plants had disappeared and fish had become scarcer, and along with them went the wading birds—spoonbills, wood storks, herons and anhinga, to name a few.

In February 2008, plans and designs were drawn for a project to fix the damage done to the wetlands by the C-111 canal. Plans were approved in September 2009, and the project was completed in 2012. With the use of pump stations, waterways and reservoirs, the C-111 Spreader Canal Western Component project is designed to hold rain water and natural flows into Taylor Slough, a critical flow path that carries water through the heart of the Everglades National Park into Florida Bay. Water is then able to flow and filter into the ground, rehydrating this wetland habitat.

Just a year after the project was put into motion, scientists began to see a positive impact on the ecosystem. Underwater plants, which form the base of Florida Bay's food chain, covered five times the area than that found in 2008. Tests also showed that the water in Florida Bay was less salty and that Taylor Slough had more water, allowing it to maintain its peat soil. If this continues, it will mean more fish and, in turn, more wading birds, followed by crocodiles and alligators.

As for the abandoned facility, the General Processing Building was demolished, most of it scrapped as the building was mostly made of metals. SFWMD has also blocked many entrances to the buildings by moving large mounds of dirt and boulders in front of the doorways. Up until 2012, some of the experimental rocket fuel could still be found in some of the pipes.

The rocket chamber used in the final test firing still sits in the firing pit to this day. Lettering on the side of the chamber reads, "SL-260-2," causing some confusion, but according to Arthur Lemaster, a former employee who worked at the Aerojet facility, the same chamber was used for both the SL-2 and SL-3 test firings. There has been a lot of interest in removing the rocket chamber and showcasing it in a museum, but none of the proposed

Above: The General Processing Building.

Below: Looking south of Aerojet Road at the main facility, which can be seen on the left.

plans has gotten very far. According to the park rangers in the area and SFWMD, anyone can have what's left of the rocket motor as long as they pay for all the expenses necessary to remove it, including the construction of a crane and transport. The shed that sat over the firing pit was dismantled, and the pit was covered up with thirty-three-ton concrete beams, essentially mothballing it in case someone does wish to preserve the chamber.

PART III

WEIRD MIAMI

Florida in general is known for having many odd and essentially weird places. On the west coast, on Marco Island, is what is now known as the Cape Romano Dome house, built to be entirely self-sufficient with the use of solar panels and an underground cistern that collects rainwater. On the east coast, on Merritt Island, was Dragon Pont Mansion, a house on the southern tip of the island with a dragon statue that overlooked the Banana River Lagoon, built by a Miami artist who claimed he was a wizard. Just north of Orlando is what is known as the Mount Dora Catacombs, a bomb shelter built by a doctor during the Cold War to hold up to twenty-five families who had reserved spots in case of a nuclear disaster.

Miami is not an exception to weird, having known oddities such as the Coral Castle in Homestead, as well as many hidden landmarks throughout the city and the Greater Miami area.

6

AMERTEC BUILDING

In 1967, Chayo Frank graduated from the University of Oklahoma with a degree in architecture and was tasked with designing an office building for his father's architectural woodworking and store fixture manufacturing business, Amertec-Granada, Inc. The office building he was tasked with constructing was to be placed in the center of the existing U-shaped factory. At just twenty-three years old and fresh from having studied under Bruce Goff, an innovator and large contributor to organic architecture, Frank set out to build what is now thought to be a hidden and unique architectural landmark in Miami.

While designing the Amertec Building, Chayo Frank did pencil compositions that consisted of studies in the use of points, lines and forms. His approach was to move in a continuous flow; no elements of the design were pre-established, and no thought was given to what should be done next. He considered every point, line and form part of a beautiful entity and ever-evolving design that was spontaneous and intuitive.

Approved by his father, the design he established developed from an approach that involved his love for the exotic beauty of tropical climates and his affinity for designing curvilinear forms. Each form was constructed by spraying concrete over "metal cages" of curved reinforcing bars and wire mesh. The water flumes on the exterior of the building were entirely free form, sculpturally connecting the primary forms of the building.

While the building was being painted, Chayo Frank began developing an idea. He wanted his design to transcend architecture as a building and become what he called an "organic entity," which involved a combination of all aspects of design to resemble an object of nature. To achieve this, he used metallic paints that enabled sunlight to reflect off the textures

Above: The Amertec Building painted white, as it has been since the 1990s.

Opposite: A shot of the staircase at the Amertec Building.

Right: The staircase inside the Amertec Building.

Above: The top floor at the Amertec Building.

Opposite: The reception area at the Amertec Building.

Below: The Amertec Building, painted in Miami Dolphins colors in 2014.

on the exterior of the building, giving it a more life-like quality.

His father's business operated until the factory and Amertec Building were sold in 1981. The building switched hands a number of times until the property was foreclosed on in 2011. Sometime in the years prior to it being foreclosed on, the metallic paints on the Amertec Building were removed and repainted white. The property was resold for $600,000 to Produce LLC in 2012.

In 2013, the exterior of the Amertec Building was repainted in different shades of orange and aqua colors. The building and surrounding factory are currently being used as storage.

7

THE REDLANDS "CORAL CASTLE" HOUSE

Old postcards called it "Coral Castle" and described how visitors were able to wander around the extensive gardens on the property surrounding the house. According to some locals, construction of the house was inspired by the sculpture garden of the same name built by Edward Leedskalnin; some local residents even claim that Leedskalnin himself built the house. However, Edward Leedskalnin did not move to Homestead until 1936, four years after this home was built.

In the 1980s, the house was owned by James Cloninger, who operated Cloninger Air Boats in the workshop just south of the property and an agricultural field to the west.

Though the exterior was relatively undamaged when Hurricane Andrew passed through South Florida in 1994, the interior was completely destroyed, along with the roof and second floor, leaving only a shell of a building.

In later years, the property would be used by other businesses. In 2005, Castlerock Nursery moved in, and then in 2012, Wicked Sisters Magical Produce set up a fruit and vegetable stand in front of the Coral Castle house. In 2011, James Cloninger passed away, leaving his estate to his family.

The property, which included a two-bedroom, two-bathroom remodeled home; a large workshop; a separate office/efficiency unit; and the Coral Castle house, was sold on March 2, 2015, for an estimated $1 million. There are no future plans for the Coral Castle house.

Above: A house that used to be called Coral Castle.

Opposite, bottom: Inside Coral Castle.

8

HOMESTEAD UFO HOUSE

Located in Homestead, just a couple miles from the Everglades Park main entrance, was a saucer-shaped, pink house, condemned and vandalized after years of not being lived in. It was called by many names, including the "Flying Saucer Home," the "UFO Home" and the "Mushroom House," all referring to the unique shape of the home. Some claim a mob boss actually built the house, making it easy for drug drops in the area. A less believable theory is that a nude colony settled there so its members could live in solitude without being bothered by neighbors. Actual information on this place is pretty scarce, though.

Designed by Miami architect Peter Vander Klout, the house was built in 1974, during a time when people were influenced by the onset of the space age and the ideas of what the world would look like in the future. Built out of concrete, the top portion was constructed first and weighed over 280 tons alone. After it was completed, the top portion was raised with the use of hydraulic rams to its final position. Pylons were put in place below to support the structure, and the walls were then built around the exterior.

Other homes designed by Peter Vander Klout in this style still exist today throughout the United States, including one in Plantation, Florida; one in Garden City, South Carolina; and another in Mettawa, Illinois. Though all were built and designed in a similar manner, the house in Homestead differed from the others because it had two units, instead of one, built adjacent to each other.

Many stories surrounded the house and its previous owners, mostly fabricated by the local teens who frequented the home after its abandonment. Some claim the house was built and owned by a gentleman who was licensed to import and export wild and exotic animals, such as lions, tigers and monkeys. It was later found that he was actually

Above, top: The kitchen on the second floor of the Mushroom House. *Bottom*: The house locals called the Mushroom House, or the UFO House, with a fountain in the foreground.

Opposite, top: A shot of the Mushroom House with both halves of the house in frame. *Bottom*: The top floor of the Mushroom House.

delivering heroin and cocaine by hiding them in a compartment underneath the animal cages. The high price of the animal would mostly go unnoticed when the actual product being sold was drugs.

The house was sold by its original owner in 2001 and switched hands only once more before being bought by a doctor from Brooklyn, New York, in 2005. It was hardly lived in and was neglected over the following years, attracting the attention of locals and vandals alike. After numerous unpaid fines and code violations against the owner of the house, the city went ahead and demolished it in August 2013.

PART IV

VICE AND GREED

On July 11, 1979, a white Ford Econoline van drove slowly through the parking lot of Dadeland Mall in Kendal—Miami's largest mall—and pulled up in front of Crown's Liquors. Not long after, a white Mercedes sedan with black tinted bulletproof windows parked nearby, driven by twenty-two-year-old Juan Carlos Hernández and thirty-seven-year-old Jiménez Panesso, one of Miami's top cocaine dealers.

Hernández and Panesso walked into the liquor store followed by two men from the Ford van. One of the men walked up to Panesso and pulled out a .380 Beretta handgun with a silencer, shooting the cocaine dealer four times in the face. Hernandez and the store clerk began running as the other gunman sprayed the store with a .45 MAC-10 machine pistol. The two assailants then walked back to the van and jumped in. As they sped away, they fired their weapons out of the back of the van, breaking store windows, damaging cars and sending shoppers running for their lives.

Dubbed the "Cocaine Cowboys," these men's actions marked the beginning of South Florida's bloody and violent drug wars during the 1980s and early '90s. In 1980, *TIME* magazine named Miami the nation's "crime capital of the world." The murder rate in Miami grew every year, with half of the killings being drug related. The mob-style executions and growing violence in the streets were linked to the Medellín Cartel, fighting for control of the quickly growing drug business.

The drug industry brought billions of dollars into Miami, which was funneled through front organizations and into the local economy. During that time, demand rose for legitimate jobs in the banking, real estate, construction and service industries. Over ten thousand building permits were issued, including to luxury car dealerships, five-star hotels, condominiums, office buildings and other major commercial developments. Any building in Miami constructed during the 1980s, especially skyscrapers such as the Southeast Financial Center, was more than likely indirectly financed by the drug industry.

After investigating, the federal government concluded that the local police departments were mostly ineffective and outside intervention was needed to get the violence and drug trafficking under control. President Ronald Reagan formed the South Florida Drug Task Force and assigned George Bush to lead a federal offensive against the Colombian drug lords. In the early '90s, as law enforcement pushed out the cartels, the large influx of cash flowing into the city stopped, causing many businesses to close.

Today, crime is nowhere near as bad as it was during the Cocaine Cowboys era, but it exists in some form, be it corruption or stealing money from the government.

PARKWAY WEST REGIONAL MEDICAL CENTER

Built in 1972, the International Medical Center (IMC) officially opened in 1974 as an eleven-story hospital with 127 rooms and enough beds to accommodate over three hundred patients, located just off the Golden Glades interchange in North Miami.

Since its establishment, local doctors and patients complained to federal regulators about the abysmal conditions of the clinics owned by IMC—one office in Little Haiti was said to not even have drapes to cover gynecological patients. Previous employees also spoke about rumors involving South American mafia members being treated under heavy security on the top floor of the hospital in North Miami.

New federal rules required firms to get special waivers if more than half of their business came from Medicare patients. Almost eight out of ten IMC patients were on Medicare, and a temporary waiver granted to IMC three years earlier was set to expire. By 1984, the accumulated complaints from doctors opposing the renewal of IMC's waiver had prompted a federal investigation into the center's operations.

Miguel G. Recarey, president and chairman of the board at IMC, employed Jeb Bush as a real estate consultant and paid him a $75,000 fee to find the company a new location, although the move never took place. Jeb Bush lobbied the Reagan administration on behalf of Recarey in regards to renewing the waiver, which allowed IMC to continue operating "as is" for a couple more years.

A Cuban exile, Recarey stood out during the excesses of the crime epidemic occurring in Miami in the 1970s and '80s. He collected assault rifles, had his office wired with sophisticated eavesdropping equipment and always traveled with heavy security by his side. He also often boasted about his ties to Tampa crime boss Santo Trafficante Jr.

After an extensive investigation, it was found that Miguel G. Recarey was stealing untold millions of dollars and believed that he used IMC to increase his net worth from $1 million to $100 million in just six years. By the time the organization collapsed in 1987, Recarey and IMC were receiving a $30 million check each month from the federal government.

In 1987, Miguel Recarey was named in three separate federal indictments. He was accused of paying $115,000 in bribes and kickbacks to top officials with the Hotel and Restaurant Employees International Union to persuade them to sign an HMO contract with IMC. He was charged with illegally wiretapping telephones and offices at his company to identify who might have been cooperating with federal investigators. Lastly, he was charged with using $355,000 in Medicare money to pay legal bills and fees.

Despite denying the charges, Recarey fled to Caracas, Venezuela, where he lived openly in a suburb called El Llanito. Federal agents were able to track him down at least four times, but he managed to get away each time. Prosecutors suspect he survived in Venezuela by bribing government officials, who would tip him off whenever federal agents were coming. Recarey later moved to Madrid, where he married a Spaniard and became a Spanish citizen. He currently remains a fugitive in Spain, where

a court denied U.S. requests for extradition.

Meanwhile, International Medical Center Inc. collapsed in 1987, mired in over $390 million in unpaid claims and debts. The clinics and hospitals owned by the organization were taken over by the government.

The hospital in North Miami changed ownership that same year and was renamed Golden Glades Regional Medical Center. It changed hands in again in 1991 and became Parkway West Regional Medical Center. It remained operational until finally closing in 2002. The property was bought in 2004 for $4.2 million by Jacob Sopher, president of Ace Parking Management.

In 2009, a group of local businessmen had plans to renovate the deteriorating hospital into an assisted living facility. It was to be named Diamond Pointe and was to have 150 rooms and fifty to one hundred employees. The $22 million project never came to fruition.

As the building deteriorated over the years, it attracted taggers, scrappers and urban explorers. The walls are covered in crude graffiti, large pieces of metal hang from the ceiling as ceiling tiles litter the floors on every level and the smell of mold is everywhere. Some people who have visited the hospital during its abandonment claim the vandalism has gotten so bad that a security guard stays on site, firing blank shots into the air to scare off any would-be trespassers entering the property.

Police have nabbed trespassers, and liens have mounted to nearly $2 million in code violations. The mayor stated in November 2010 that it was apparent how bad the building had gotten.

The new owner, BSD of Miami Gardens, has begun planning to resurrect the building. Trustee Yaniz Nakash said the company would gut the building and then build commercial and residential units. Plans stumbled when the property was put into foreclosure over a $3 million mortgage. The foreclosure was released after BSD signed a second mortgage for $300,000. As of 2015, though security has been placed on site and police cruisers now patrol the area looking for would-be trespassers, no progress has been made on the building itself.

10

SOUTH SHORE HOSPITAL AND MEDICAL CENTER

Located at the corner of Alton Road and West Sixth Street, South Shore Hospital and Medical Center was built in 1967 to serve the surrounding area.

By 2002, the hospital was $30 million in debt and was losing up to $31 million a year. Developer Crescent Heights purchased the property in February 2004 and planned to renovate the building and change it from a nonprofit hospital to a for-profit one. The initial plan was to sell the property to David Galbut, the brother of Crescent Heights managing principal Russell Galbut, and rename the hospital South Beach Doctor's Hospital.

A fifty-five-thousand-square-foot condo building was planned for just north of the hospital, followed by tearing down the nearby Stanley Meyers Health Clinic and building a thirty-five-square-foot condo building. The complex would be dubbed the South Beach Professional Center.

The plan fell through, however, and the hospital was sold to nursing home operator Dr. Ira S. Barton and longtime South Shore administrator William Zubkoff; they signed a thirty-five-year lease with Crescent Heights in March 2005 and renamed the medical center South Beach Community Hospital. At this time, the hospital had also been consolidated into the three-story building while still operating with 148 beds, leaving the connected ten-story structure vacant.

In December, the hospital was threatened with exclusion from participation in Medicare, Medicaid and all other federal care programs if it didn't comply with its corporate integrity agreement. This came after previous owners settled charges of over-billing Medicare with false reports.

Right: Medical equipment in the surgical wing of South Shore Hospital.

Opposite, top: An MRI machine on one of the upper floors of South Shore Hospital.

Opposite, bottom: A bed inside the Pediatric Wing at South Shore Hospital.

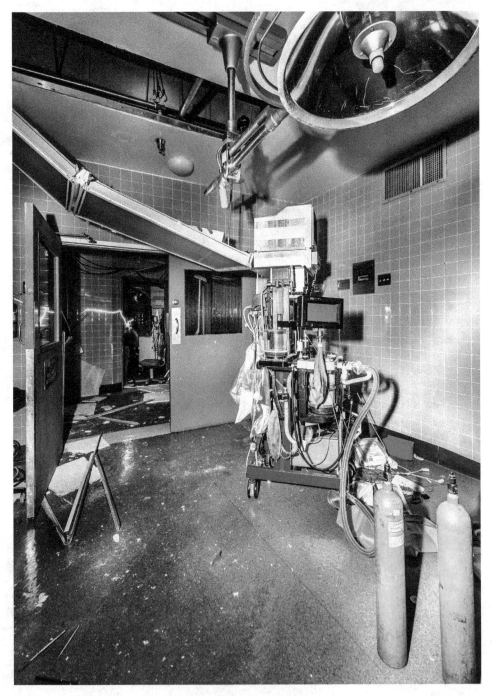

A surgery room at South Shore Hospital.

Opposite: An X-ray machine in South Shore Hospital.

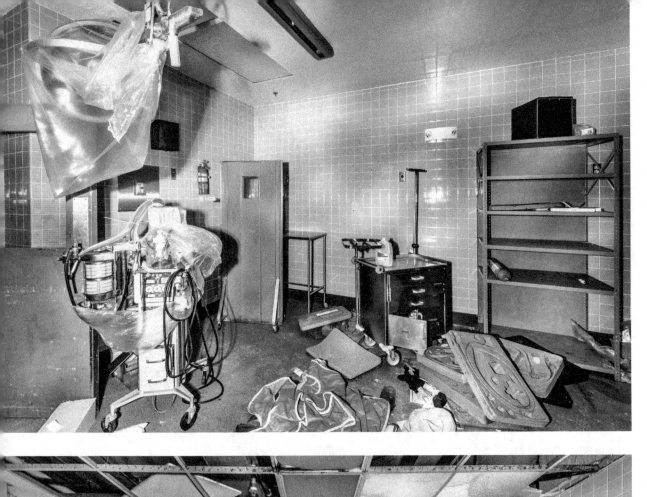

In March 2006, the owners filed for Chapter 11 bankruptcy protection, listing no assets and debts totaling more than $5.3 million. They sold the property in June.

The hospital remained empty until 2011, when developer and owner Crescent Heights began plans to demolish the structure, along with a convenience store across the street and a nearby parking garage, to replace it with a residential condo tower.

Opposite, top: A surgery room at South Shore Hospital.

Opposite, bottom: One of the ER rooms in South Shore Hospital.

11

DOROTHY WALKER BUSH GREAT FLORIDIAN 2000

THE DIRECT ORIENT EXPRESS ICE CREAM PARLOR

Railroad Car 2409 was built in 1912 by the Pullman Company as a palace car for the Richmond, Fredericksburg and Potomac Railroad Line to carry dignitaries between Richmond, Virginia, and Washington, D.C. It was rebuilt in the 1920s and again in the 1930s with the addition of air conditioning.

During World War II, it underwent another change in look and personality when it was sold to the Clyde Beatty Circus as a pie car, where performers or crew members could buy food such as soda, chips or ice cream during their free time. The car was moved to Fort Lauderdale, where the circus maintained winter headquarters on Sunrise Boulevard at what is now the Gateway Shopping Center.

In the 1950s, the car was sold again to Royal American Shows, at the time the largest midway in North America. Still used as a pie car, it spent its last thirty working years traveling from the carnival's winter headquarters in Tampa to state fairs in the Midwest and Canada. In the early 1980s, railroad costs rose, prompting Royal American to switch to trucks and retire the railroad car.

The car sat derelict in the Tampa woods until Richard Winer, known for his books on haunted houses and the Bermuda Triangle, found and bought it for $3,500 in 1983. He moved it by rail to a siding at William Thies and Sons, a beer distribution plant in Wilton Manors, Florida, and began work on it in November 1986.

After completing its restoration in 1987, he convinced the Fort Lauderdale City Commission that Car 2409 would complement the planned River Walk and help keep people downtown, and he opened the Direct Orient Express ice cream parlor at 150 West Broward Boulevard. Two years later, he was

Inside the Direct Orient Express ice cream parlor.

Opposite: A passenger room inside the Direct Orient Express ice cream parlor.

evicted to make room for a 1,200-car parking garage and moved the railroad car into storage.

THE GENERAL MYER AND MORN

Built out of an old hospital car in 1951, the General Albert J. Myer (labeled POTUS I) SC-1 communications car replaced the older Car 1401, which always accompanied the presidential train car, Ferdinand Magellan, now on display at the Gold Coast Railroad Museum. Following the Myer was the Morn (labeled POTUS II), also built from a hospital car; this housed the living quarters for the personnel of the Myer. It included a small kitchen, bunk beds, a small bathroom with a shower and a living area. No photos of the interior of the Morn in service have been found.

The radio car was a converted hospital car and appeared to have been gutted and then built as required. There was a window installed so the operation could be viewed from the hallway that passed between the rail cars. As one sat at the console, there was a large glass window behind by the walkway to the left side of the car. Looking out that

glass window past the walkway was another large glass window on the car body. If anyone on the platform were to look into the car window, he or she would see the whole console and operators.

The radio car had to be placed on the tracks so it faced the hospital car because of the coax connectors on the front end. The train had to be configured with the hospital car toward the train engine and the radio or communications car following. The coax connectors on the hospital car were connected by coax jumpers to the coax connectors on the communications car. This was also because, on the opposite end (from the coax connector end), there were connectors that carried audio to the end of the train.

When the Ferdinand Magellan was taken out of service in 1958, the two communication cars were moved to the New Cumberland Army Depot in Harrisburg, Pennsylvania, in the 1960s and '70s. The rail cars made their last official trip when President Kennedy went to the Army-Navy football game in Philadelphia in 1961.

The POTUS I train car, aka the General Myer.

A storage room in the General Myer.

Opposite, top: A hallway inside the passenger car of the General Myer.

Opposite, bottom: Inside the General Myer communications train car.

THE GREAT TRAIN HEIST

In 2005, Tony Campos, project director at the Hollywood Railroad Station Museum, was tasked with creating a train to commemorate Dorothy Walker Bush, the late grandmother of President George W. Bush and former Florida governor Jeb Bush. It was to be named the Dorothy Walker Bush Great Floridian 2000. The train was to include the 1924 FEC Engine 253, the Myer and Morn, a mail car used in *Buffalo Bill's Wild West Show*, a Jim Crow–era car and the Direct Orient Express ice cream parlor. He was granted $375,000 by the Florida Division of Historical Resources and was expected to have the cars ready for display by June 2006.

In 2006, Campos acknowledged that the restoration wasn't going to be completed on time and cited as contributing factors hurricanes, a break-in, sketchy historical documents, lack of grant money and a PBS documentary crew's delay in

The *Buffalo Bill* mail car.

Opposite, top: Inside a Jim Crow–era baggage train car.

Opposite, bottom: Inside the *Buffalo Bill* mail car.

filming the project. In October 2006, the Florida Division of Historical Resources sent a letter to Campos asking about the expenditure of the grant money. Campos never responded to the letter, stopped answering phone calls and was hardly ever at his office at the station. It was requested that he return the money or face legal action; he failed to comply and was arrested soon after.

What's left of the failure of a project now sits rotting away behind a South Florida warehouse. Two train cars thought to be presidential cars, with the names POTUS I and POTUS II stenciled on the sides, sit on wood blocks at the front of the tracks. Attached are the 1918 *Buffalo Bill's Wild West Show* postal car, the Direct Orient Express ice cream parlor and a Jim Crow–era car that carried a baggage compartment to separate black passengers from whites on the rest of the train.

There has been interest by multiple parties to acquire the train cars, but due to local vandals and graffiti taggers, their condition has degraded immensely, causing any interest there was to vanish. Graffiti covers the inside and outside of the cars, holes riddle the floor from

where scrappers have cut their way
in and there is a lack of windows
while the ones that do remain have
bullet holes in them.

PART V

PRESERVATION

"Demolition by neglect" is a term used for a situation in which a property owner intentionally allows a historic property to suffer severe deterioration, potentially beyond the point of repair. Property owners may use this kind of long-term neglect to circumvent historic preservation regulations.

The term is usually brought up when an owner has an abandoned property listed on the National Register of Historic Places. These sites can be difficult to demolish due to the fact that they are meant to be preserved, and strict guidelines must be followed if renovation is attempted. The owner can apply for a demolition permit as many times as he would like, but he will usually be denied. Though the property can't be demolished, it doesn't mean there has to be any upkeep either, so the owner decides to let the building run its course.

After a couple fires, some water damage and a bit of graffiti, the owner has succeeded; the place has become an eyesore and a danger to the community. After complaints from neighbors who are tired of kids throwing parties there or vagrants coming in and out of the property, the owner now has the community's support when he decides to apply for yet another demolition permit.

This situation is sadly more common than most would think here in Florida, and those properties that are secured and mothballed are usually tied up in legal disputes, prolonging the preservation process. Thankfully, the City of Miami has been working toward preserving some of its historical landmarks. Though there is still much work to be done, progress is being made.

12

COCONUT GROVE PLAYHOUSE

Originally constructed as a movie theater, the Coconut Grove Theater was built by Irving J. Thomas and Fin L. Pierce of the Thomas-Pierce Holding Company and designed by Richard Kiehnel of the renowned architecture firm Kiehnel and Elliot. Ground was broken for the new theater on January 7, 1926, at the corner of Main Highway and Charles Street in Coconut Grove.

Richard Kiehnel (1870–1944) was born in Germany and studied at the University of Breslau and at the École des Beaux-Arts in Paris. In 1906, he began an architectural firm with John B. Elliot in Pittsburgh, Pennsylvania, and was named the designer, while Elliot oversaw the construction of the projects.

Kiehnel's first commission in the Miami area was in 1917, a mansion dubbed "El Jardin" built for John Bindley, president of the Pittsburgh Steel Company. Departing from the Mission style that had only recently appeared in Florida, Kiehnel designed the mansion in the Mediterranean Revival style. It is noted as being the earliest Mediterranean Revival work in South Florida.

Many of his and his firm's works are listed on the National Register of Historic Places. Among his designs in Miami are the Coral Gables Congregational Church, Miami Senior High School, the Seybold Building and Arcade and the Scottish Rite Temple.

As part of the announcement for the Coconut Grove Theater's construction, it was promoted as having more seats than any other theater in Miami. It was renowned for being the second movie theater on the east coast of Florida to be air-conditioned and for having the largest Wurlitzer concert grand organ in the United States. The building was designed for mixed uses, having seven storefronts on the ground floor, offices on the second and apartments located on the third floor.

The Coconut Grove Playhouse.

Before its opening, the theater was turned over to Paramount Pictures Corporation. It was thought that having the theater run by Paramount would better serve the community of Coconut Grove, as it was likely to have access to more attractions. The Coconut Grove Theater was the eleventh Paramount theater in southeastern Florida and would open under the Publix Theaters Corporation, an exhibiting organization under Paramount Pictures.

On January 1, 1927, the theater had its opening night, which featured D.W. Griffith's production of *The Sorrows of Satan*, headlined by actor Adolf Menjou. Arnold Johnson and Celia Santon accompanied the movie with a twelve-piece orchestra played on the Wurlitzer organ. The theater was packed for both showings of the film, accommodating 1,500 people per showing. Reverend J.D. Kuykendall of Plymouth Congregational Church addressed the audience, comparing the growth of the movie picture industry with the growth of the city of Coconut Grove.

The theater couldn't have opened at a worse possible time. Florida was in a poor financial state as the real estate market had crashed around 1925, causing many real estate investors to liquidate their holdings or to go bankrupt under crushing mortgage debt. In 1933, Paramount went into receivership and declared bankruptcy in 1935. The Coconut Grove Theater managed to stay open until the mid-1930s. After its closure, the building was used during World War II as a school to train air force navigators.

TRANSFORMATION

Following the war, the building was shuttered until 1955, when oil magnate George Engle purchased the old theater for $200,000 with the intent of creating Miami's first live and legitimate performing arts theater. At an estimated cost of $700,000, Engle hired local architect Alfred Browning Parker to renovate the theater, which had fallen into disrepair after having been shuttered for so many years.

Alfred Browning Parker (1916–2011) was born in Boston, Massachusetts, and moved to Miami when he was eight years old. Parker received his bachelor's of science in architecture at the University of Florida in 1939 and served as an associate professor at the school from 1942 to 1946. Realizing the importance of practicing to establish himself as a seasoned architect, Parker moved his family to Coconut Grove, where he began his own architectural firm.

Parker designed commercial, religious and institutional buildings but is noted most for his residential

Seating inside the Coconut Grove Playhouse.

designs. Influenced by Frank Lloyd Wright, Parker designed and built over 6,400 projects in his lifetime and made a name for himself as a modernist architect who created unique dwellings that embraced their local environments. In 1959, Frank Lloyd Wright himself recommended Parker as an American Institute of Architects Fellow, an honor that recognizes architects who have achieved a standard of excellence in architecture at both the local and national levels and who have made a significant contribution to both architecture and society. Parker was the only architect recommended by Wright.

Throughout the 1960s, '70s and '80s, Parker's designs were featured in many architectural magazines. Once a year, *House Beautiful* magazine dedicated an entire issue to one home that it chose as House of the Year; four of Parker's houses were selected. In 2006, *Wall Paper* magazine chose Parker's Woodsong residence in Miami for its "Top 10 Houses of the World"—the only house chosen in North America.

Renamed the Coconut Grove Playhouse, the newly renovated theater opened on January 3,

The stage entrance at Coconut Grove Playhouse.

1956, with the U.S. premiere of Samuel Beckett's *Waiting for Godot*, billed as "the laugh sensation of two continents," starring Bert Lahr and Tom Ewell. The performance bombed, with audience members walking out in large numbers and critics calling it "the dirtiest, most obscene, pornographic" show they had ever seen. The next day, there was a line going all the way down the street with people waiting to get their money back for the previous night's performance. In a house built for 1,200, only 48 people were in the audience for the second night.

Engle closed the theater in 1960 after many disappointing years in terms of financial success and attracting audiences. Between 1964 and 1965, the theater was occupied by the Miami Actors Company, which was to be an extension of the National Theatre and Academy. The effort was launched by Ilse Earl, who taught playhouse groups at Miami-Dade. Out of more than one hundred people who tried out, only twenty actors and performers from Miami and the surrounding areas were chosen to be part of this important event. Shows included *J.B.* by Archibald MacLeish, *All the Way Home* by Tad Model and *Slow Dance on the Killing Ground* by William Hanley, which was a rushed substitution for *Hogan's Goat*, having been put in place with only ten days of rehearsals.

The building was purchased in 1966 by producer Zev Buffman for more than $1 million. It changed ownership again in 1970, when it was bought by former actor Eddie Bracken and his associates. When Bracken's group failed to pay its debts, the playhouse was ordered to be sold at auction.

Broadway producers Arthur Cantor and Robert Fishko bought the theater and reopened it for the 1971–72 winter season. They saw much success throughout their years running the theater, most notably with their production of *Equus* in 1975. In 1977, Cantor and Fishko sold their interest to the Player's Repertory Company, a semiprofessional community theater that performed at the Museum of Science. Player's hired Robert Kantor as artistic director when it moved to the Coconut Grove Playhouse, renaming it the Player's State Theater and becoming one of three state theaters in Florida. Kantor brought in executive director David Black, who had formerly managed the Public Theatre in New York and Trinity Square in Providence. Going into the 1980s, the name was changed back to the Coconut Grove Playhouse, and José Ferrer replaced Kantor as artistic director in 1982.

Opposite: A mannequin inside one of the offices on the top floor of the Coconut Grove Playhouse.

Under Ferrer's guidance and direction, the playhouse gained a reputation as one of the nation's leading theaters. In 1985, Arnold Mittelman replaced Ferrer as artistic director. Among the productions that premiered here prior to a Broadway opening were Neil Simon's *The Sunshine Boys*, starring Jack Klugman and Tony Randall, and *Urban Cowboy*. Sherry Glaser's *Family Secrets* moved to off-Broadway and became the theater's longest-running one-woman show. The playhouse presented the world premiere of *Fame: The Musical*, which went on to great success in Baltimore, Philadelphia and London's West End, and mounted a revival of *Death of a Salesman*, starring Hal Holbrook and Elizabeth Franz, prior to a national tour.

The State of Florida acquired the playhouse in 1980 by purchasing its $1.5 million mortgage and contracted Coconut Grove Playhouse Inc. to operate it. In 2004, the state transferred the title to Coconut Grove Playhouse Inc. with the requirement that it be operated as a theater.

The theater was celebrating fifty years in 2006 when it was

The stage of the Coconut Grove Playhouse. A sign for *Sonia Flew*, the last play at the theater, can be seen.

A close-up view of the main entrance to the Coconut Grove Playhouse. The neon sign still hangs on the side.

abruptly shuttered in April because the board feared its liability insurance had expired. During that time, news got out about a $4 million deficit. The theater reopened its doors a week later, and amid news of mounting debt, it was announced that the final show of its current season, *Sonia Flew*, would indeed go on. After a pledge of $50,000 by lead actress Lucie Arnaz to match the same amount made by Bacardi Liquors and a reported $25,000 from relatives of Arnold Mittelman, the artistic director, *Sonia Flew* ran for just ten days of its scheduled four-week run. The theater closed afterward.

After years of Coconut Grove Playhouse Inc. being unable to revitalize the facility and failure to keep it running as a theater, as well as allowing a commercial parking venture on the property, the state retook ownership in 2012. In August 2013, Governor Rick Scott and the Florida cabinet approved a joint plan by Florida International University and Miami-Dade County mayor Carlos Gimenez to reopen the playhouse as a working theater.

Under the plan, the county would rebuild the theater using $20 million in previously approved bond and bed-tax money. The playhouse will be built as a three-hundred-seat theater operated by GableStage, a theater group based out of the Biltmore Hotel, with space devoted to theater classes provided by Florida International University. According to a roughly estimated schedule by the county, construction is not expected to start until October 2017, and the work is expected to be finished by September 30, 2019.

13

CRANDON PARK ZOO

In late August and early September 1965, a hurricane spun across the Atlantic Ocean, looping, pausing and backtracking like some terrible ballerina trying to keep her audience guessing at the final act. For a while, it looked as if Hurricane Betsy would pass Florida altogether, but off Jacksonville, she performed one of her loops and turned back toward the Bahamas.

On September 6, 1965, Labor Day, Miami's radar began to pick up the eye wall, and on the seventh, the National Weather Bureau warned of storm tides six to ten feet above normal in coastal areas. That warning would be far too late to protect the animals locked inside their cages at the Crandon Park Zoo on Key Biscayne. On September 8, as Betsy made landfall near Key Largo, more than three feet of water poured into the zoo. Many animals drowned while locked inside their concrete and steel cages, while others died of

panic. In total, 250 of the zoos 1,000 animals died during the storm.

Betsy moved through Florida and into the Gulf, headed toward landfall in Louisiana, where it would leave more than seventy dead. Eventually, Hurricane Betsy would be titled "Billion-Dollar Betsy" because it was the first hurricane to cause more than $1 billion in damages. In her destruction, she would be the beginning of the end for the seaside zoo located on Key Biscayne.

Once owners of one of the largest coconut plantations in the United States, the Matheson family, among the pioneers in the area, donated the entire north end of Key Biscayne to the Miami-Dade County for the creation of a park to be open to the public in 1940. One of the stipulations of the donation was that the county would build a causeway from the mainland to the park. Almost immediately, there were accusations that the Matheson

family had used the donation to secure the construction of a bridge that would vastly increase the value of their holdings still on the island, but critics aside, the roughly nine hundred acres would indeed become a park.

A Zoo in the Tropics

The Japanese attack on Pearl Harbor and America's entrance into World War II delayed the construction of the causeway due to shortages of materials and labor, but in 1947, the Rickenbacker Causeway and the park opened to the public. The park would be called Crandon Park after Commissioner Charles H. Crandon, who arranged construction of the causeway.

One of the park's features that would become a favorite of locals and garner international recognition came about by a sort of happy accident. In 1948, a traveling show became disabled and subsequently sold

The Bird Aviary at Crandon Park.

A monkey cage at Crandon Park.

some of its animals to the county. The Crandon Park Zoo opened with two bears, three monkeys and a goat purchased from the circus. Slowly, the collection began to grow through gifts and the purchase of animals, creating one of the most unique zoos in America overlooking the clear blue waters of the Atlantic Ocean.

Through the 1950s and into the early 1960s, the zoo continued to grow and expand. The addition of a small train that would take visitors on a one-and-a-half-mile trip around the zoo and through the lush tropical vegetation would make a lasting impression on the younger zoo-goers. Many locals have fond memories of riding the train with family and friends. It was a highlight of any trip to the zoo. Likewise, the creation of a small animal petting zoo would cement Crandon Park and the zoo as favorite destinations for locals and tourists alike.

The idyllic tropical zoo would not escape controversy. Beginning in 1960 and periodically after, local news outlets would run stories alleging animal abuse and cruelty, mostly stemming from the concrete and steel-bar enclosures in which the animals were confined. Public opinions and attitudes toward how zoos should treat their animals on exhibit were beginning to change.

The controversy did not stop Crandon Park Zoo from becoming one of the most popular. In 1965, with one thousand animals on display, it was recognized as one of the major zoos in the country. The tragedy of Hurricane Betsy would be a crushing blow. While events were set in motion that would eventually see the animals moved to a new facility, the staff at Crandon Park Zoo rebuilt and started back to work, generating a list of accomplishments that would raise the status of the zoo and the area.

In 1967, with more than 1,200 animals, Crandon Park Zoo was considered one the top twenty-five zoos in the United States. Also that year, it was successful in breeding its two Asian elephants, Dahlip and Seetna, giving birth to two offspring—an extremely rare accomplishment even today.

The year 1968 saw the second white tiger ever brought to the United States, and in 1970, the zoo acquired the rarest of its inhabitants: a pair of Indian rhinos. Also, the first key deer ever removed from the Key Deer National Wildlife Refuge was placed on display.

Monkey cages at Crandon Park.

Then, in 1973, two bald eagles were hatched in captivity, marking the first instance of a successful hatching anywhere in nearly fifty years.

With the growth of the zoo, public opinion toward the concrete animal enclosures and the constant fear of another hurricane, the decision was made that the zoo needed to be moved from its present location to a safer area. With that in mind, when the former Richmond Naval Air Station became available in 1970, Miami-Dade made a formal request for the property. The idea was that its location to the southwest of Miami would provide protection for the zoo and the animals in the event of another hurricane and also more room for expansion. Construction began in 1975 with the creation of a large moat. Meanwhile, Crandon Park Zoo continued to grow its collection of animals and expand its exhibits, and families flocked from all around the area to experience the zoo.

Big cat cages at Crandon Park.

MOVING LOCATIONS

The new zoo would first open with the Preview Center and twelve exhibits in 1980. The Miami Metro Zoo officially opened on December 12, 1981, with the addition of the Asia Exhibit. The opening of the new zoo in the southwest part of the county would mark the end of the Crandon Park Zoo. Guests would no longer ride the train or be able to enjoy the ocean vistas while observing animals in cages.

The southwestern zoo also marked an end to something else. The Miami Metro Zoo would be one of the first free-range zoos in the United States. Animals would no longer be kept in cages, and as a symbol of that commitment, guests at the zoo's opening were given a gift of small pieces of steel bars cut from the animal cages at Crandon Zoo. These were called "Pieces of the Past."

Miami Metro Zoo would grow to be a jewel of Miami-Dade County

The back of the monkey cages at Crandon Park, where the zookeepers would feed them.

A monkey cage at Crandon Park.

and Florida, but sadly, Mother Nature would give a reminder that just because you are not located along the ocean does not mean you are safe from a raging hurricane. On August 24, 1992, Hurricane Andrew came ashore near Homestead and ravaged the whole of South Florida, including the zoo. Trees were downed, roofs were torn from exhibits and fences were destroyed. Tragically, one hundred exotic birds were killed when the aviary collapsed. In total, Andrew would be responsible for the loss of three antelopes, one ostrich, one gibbon and the birds, but the devotion of the staff, the generosity of the community and the lessons of the past prevented more catastrophic losses to the zoo population.

Today, Crandon Park remains a popular destination, with tennis courts, beaches, a golf course, the Marjory Stoneman Douglas Biscayne Nature Center, a marina and much more. A member of the Matheson family still sits on the board for the park. Unfortunately, the Mathesons and the county have been involved in legal wrangling from time to time over the direction and management of the park.

The Crandon Zoo location is now a botanical garden where visitors can roam among lush tropical vegetation. Some of the old cages remain as a reminder of its history and how the animals were once kept.

Miami Metro Zoo is now called Zoo Miami and has become one of the foremost zoos in the country, with more than three thousand animals of five hundred species, forty of which are endangered. It also boasts more than one thousand types of trees and plants, a children's area, a petting zoo, playgrounds and a monorail circling the 750-acre park that evokes memories of a small train on Key Biscayne that ran around a small beach-side zoo.

14

MIAMI MARINE STADIUM

In 1962, the City of Miami hired the Chicago firm of Ralph H. Burke to create a master plan for a new park on Virginia Key, along the Rickenbacker Causeway. The proposal called for a monumental racecourse for speedboats, similar to Rome's Circus Maximus but with water. It would include a grandstand on the south side and be open to Biscayne Bay on the northwest end.

The inclusion of a grandstand and other amenities for a large audience came at a time when boat racing and water skiing were exploding in popularity throughout the country. Amateurs and professionals alike embraced a sport that had once been accessible only to the wealthy who owned yachts or belonged to private clubs. Yet no city in America had an adequate boat-racing course. In Miami, the annual Orange Bowl Regatta in December attracted hundreds of spectators and boat entries, but due to the lack of unprotected and limited space, the event also gained public criticism.

The new stadium was to be the world's first arena specifically designed for powerboat racing. Though other marine stadiums existed, such as the Long Beach Marine Stadium in California or the Jones Beach Marine Theatre in New York, each was built for either rowing/boat races or musical concerts. Miami's new stadium would capitalize on tourism and local revenue with a diverse list of events to be hosted on site, including major regattas, shows and concerts.

The City of Miami hired the Miami-based architectural firm of Pancoast, Ferendino, Skeels and Burnham, as well as Dignum Engineers, to carry out the project. Dignum's lead engineer, Jack Meyer, and a young Cuban-born architect named Hilario Candela from Pancoast, Ferendino, set out to construct an outstanding piece of architecture—a sculptural piece.

THE ARCHITECT

At twenty-seven years old, Hilario Candela had a résumé of experiences prior to this project on which he usefully drew for the stadium. Candela trained at the Georgia Institute of Technology, where he had the opportunity to meet and work alongside some of the most influential architects in concrete design, including Italian architect Pier Luigi Nervi, Spanish structural engineer Eduardo Torroja and Spanish-Mexican architect Félix Candela.

After graduation, Candela returned to Havana, Cuba, where he interned under Max Borges Jr., designer of the famed Arcos de Cristal at the Tropicana Night Club, and Sáenz, Cancio, Martín, Álvarez and Gutiérrez—the largest firm in Havana at the time. It was here that Candela was introduced to thin-shell concrete construction, which he would later use in the construction of the Miami Marine Stadium. He traveled back to Miami to join Pancoast, Ferendino, Skeels and Burnham, where his first project was to construct a series of buildings for the first campus of Miami-Dade College.

A wide shot of the Miami Marine Stadium with Miami's downtown area in the background.

A close-up of the seat numbering at the Miami Marine Stadium.

The City of Miami wasn't looking for anything special or unique; it wanted something along the lines of a baseball stadium, something made of steel. Seeing that the salt air and water would quickly damage the structure if it were constructed from steel, Hilario Candela, who was just five years out of school, proposed constructing the stadium out of concrete, with part of it hanging out over the water. Inspired by Eduardo Torroja's horse track, the Zarzuela Hippodrome in Madrid, his vision was for a concrete structure that was symbolic, a place for community engagement, with a roof that took inspiration from the sailboats and water.

Miami's Department of Public Works, known for erecting practical infrastructure like highways, wasn't interested in building a work of art. Wanting the stadium built for no more than $1 million, it wasn't too enthralled with the plan proposed by Candela and the rest of his team, and it came to a point where Candela offered to build the stadium for free if it went over budget. The city accepted the deal and went ahead with Candela's plan.

A MODERN MARVEL

After six months of construction, the Commodore Ralph Middleton Munroe Marine Stadium, as it was officially named, opened on December 27, 1963, named in honor of early pioneer Ralph Munroe, a yacht designer, founder of the Biscayne Bay Yacht Club and early resident of Coconut Grove who built his home, the Barnacle, on the future site of the Barnacle Historic State Park. Despite having only a $1 million budget, the stadium was completed under budget at just $960,000.

Undoubtedly, the rooftop is the most apparent and striking aspect of the Marine Stadium. By molding the concrete, Candela and Meyer were able to construct the roofline into a series of "hyperbolic paraboloids" that are supposed to reflect on the waves made by powerful winds against the surface of the water. Having worked with Félix Candela in

A wide shot showing the entirety of the Miami Marine Stadium.

the past, Hilario Candela drew on his knowledge of thin-shell concrete in the design and construction of the roof, which is only three inches thick at some points, with galvanized steel to help support it. At 326 feet long, its 65-foot overhang is simply held up by eight columns at the rear, which provided unobstructed viewing for spectators as well. The combination of concrete and steel would contribute to the incredible stability of the Marine Stadium, which has withstood multiple hurricanes throughout the years and remains structurally sound even to this day.

Utilizing a floating stage in front of the grandstand, the seven-thousand-seat stadium was host to hundreds of events throughout the years, ranging from music concerts to boxing matches. Some major events included Jimmy Buffett's two-day performance "Live by the Bay" in August 1985, multiple performances by Gloria Estefan and the Miami Sound Machine and the famous campaign rally in 1972 when

Stadium seating at the Miami Marine Stadium.

Sammy Davis Jr. hugged President Richard Nixon.

The stadium was world renowned for featuring many world-class powerboat events, including Unlimited Hydroplane, Inboard, Outboard, Performance Craft, Stock, Modified and Grand National divisions, as well as other special event races. The stadium would become the site of a number of nationally televised events, including the Bill Muncey Invitational and the ESPN All-American Challenge Series, earning Miami the title of being the "boat racing capital of the United States."

The End of an Era

Going into the 1980s, the stadium saw a decline in events due to a number of issues, including new restrictions, political pressure from the City of Miami and a lack of promoting such events. Along with the issues mentioned, the stadium was also facing growing competition from newer venues, such as the James L. Knight Center and the Miami Arena. The last major race at the stadium was the 1987 Inboard Hydroplane national championship, and by the 1990s, powerboat racing at the stadium was nothing but a memory.

In 1992, Hurricane Andrew struck South Florida, causing billions of dollars' worth of damages. After the storm, engineers for the city allegedly found cracks in the stadium's foundation, declaring it structurally unsound. The city requested $1 million from FEMA with the purpose of demolishing the stadium after condemning the building on September 18, 1992, under Miami-Dade County building code. The insurance company hired engineering firm Simpson Gumpertz and Heger Inc. to do a study and found that the stadium had suffered no damages from Hurricane Andrew but would require $2 to $3 million for lack of maintenance throughout the years of its operation. After the study was made public, public opposition to the demolition pushed the city to back off and return the money to FEMA.

During its condemnation, the stadium became a haven for graffiti artists and was known locally as a penit. Due to a lack of security, the stadium is covered in graffiti, from quick crude tags to large elaborate pieces.

In June 2007, the city unveiled the first draft of a master plan by EDSA, a planning and landscape architecture firm, for revitalizing Virginia Key. The Marine Stadium is not in the

Opposite, top: The concession area (right) at the Miami Marine Stadium.

Opposite, bottom: Below the Miami Marine Stadium.

plan, and the two hundred people in attendance at the community meeting asked the city to include the stadium in the plan.

REVITALIZATION

On February 20, 2008, the Friends of Miami Marine Stadium (FMMS) was formed, a group supporting the restoration of the stadium founded by Hilario Candela, the original architect of the Miami Marine Stadium, and Jorge Hernández, a professor of architecture at the School of Architecture of the University of Miami.

Due to the group's efforts, the stadium has been recognized as an architectural masterpiece by the National Trust for Historic Preservation and was included in its 2009 *11 Most Endangered Historic Places*, an annual report that brings awareness and publicity to historical buildings that are in danger of being demolished or destroyed. The Marine Stadium was also named to the 2010 World Monuments Fund watch list, the foremost organization worldwide devoted to the preservation of architectural

The technical booth that hangs from the roof at the Miami Marine Stadium.

A ramp that leads to the second floor of the Miami Marine Stadium.

and cultural sites, alongside other marvels such as Machu Picchu, the historical center of Buenos Aires and the City of Old Jerusalem.

With the help of local and national organizations, including the World Monuments Fund, the National Trust for Historic Preservation, the Office of Commissioner Carlos Giménez and the John and Selene Devaney Foundation, $50,000 was raised to fund an engineering study to evaluate the condition of the structure and the cost to restore it. Simpson Gumpertz and Heger, the same firm that did the study in 1993 after Hurricane Andrew, was hired and found that renovating the stadium would cost between $5.5 and $8.5 million, which is substantially less than the $15.0 million estimate by the City of Miami in 2008.

After multiple revisions, the Miami City Commission unanimously approved a master plan for Virginia Key, which included the Miami Marine Stadium and surrounding basin. Miami-Dade County commissioners also passed a resolution to allocate $3 million to the stadium to start its historical preservation and return it as a venue for water sports and major concerts as long as all other funding was raised first.

For the next few years, FMMS would host a number of events to raise funds and awareness for the Marine Stadium, from design contents to art shows. In 2012, the stadium was named to the National Treasures list of the National Trust for Historic Preservation. The National Treasures program provides expert resources through its organization, including preservation, advocacy, legal aid, marketing and fundraising.

In May 2013, Gloria Estefan began working closely with the Friends of Miami Marine Stadium in bringing awareness and public support to its efforts to restore the stadium.

The City of Miami granted control of the stadium property to the group in 2013; it had until January 2015 to show successful fundraising and a viable operating plan to secure a long-term lease. The group was to show that the stadium, a perennial money loser when it was open, could be managed without public subsidies.

Inside one of the rooms at the Miami Marine Stadium.

It returned in late 2014 with a revitalization proposal and supposed funds.

In November 2014, FMMS and Gloria Estefan, who has been the public face of the group, announced that the Miami International Boat Show would be moving to the Miami Marine Stadium starting in 2016. The boat show would boost the stadium's finances, as it had netted the Miami Beach Convention Center $680,000 the previous year. If the city agreed to it, restoration would begin by ripping up asphalt, installing utilities and planting grass and trees so that the property would be ready by the 2016 boat show.

On November 20, 2014, FMMS presented its proposal to the Miami City Commission. The proposal would have cost about $121 million and would have brought the Miami Boat Show to the stadium, but it was shot down by the city commission after it learned that the proposal also involved extensively developing the site to add an exposition center, dry dock storage, retail and restaurants. The proposal also included a fee awarded

A wider shot of the seats at the Miami Marine Stadium.

to both Hilario Candela and Jorge Hernández.

Gloria Estefan expressed her disappointment in an open letter to the City of Miami Officials, stating:

As the public face and spokesperson for the restoration of the Miami Marine Stadium, I feel that my credibility and reputation have been put into question merely by my presumed association with the plan presented by FMMS. I had absolutely NO prior knowledge of the expansive plan that they ultimately presented to the Commission. Following the hearing, a blogger accused Emilio and me of being self-serving, suggesting we were going to profit from our preservation work by opening a restaurant at the site. Nothing could be further from the truth. Neither Emilio nor I have any agenda here other than to see this unique stadium restored, and we would never engage in activity that would so clearly be a conflict of interest and contrary to our ethical standards.

Stephanie K. Meeks, president of the National Trust for Historic Preservation, was surprised after hearing the plan as well, expecting Hilario Candela and Jorge Hernández's continued work, as it has been for the past five years, to be on a volunteer basis.

FMMS co-founder Don Worth, who was quietly against the proposed plan, stated:

I really apologize not only to Gloria but also to the National Trust for Historic Preservation and all the other groups who supported so strongly the restoration of the Marine Stadium for what was an ill-advised move. It's extremely unfortunate that seven years of very hard work and very successful interests on so many fronts has come down to this. Our credibility has taken an enormous hit, deservedly. I don't know if this group [even if] reformulated can recover from it.

After rejecting the plan, the City of Miami decided to move forward with its own plans for the stadium, working closely with the National Marine Manufacturers Association (NMMA), parent company of the International Boat Show. Under the new plan, the city would retain control of the stadium and surrounding campus while ceding daily operations to a private contractor. An $18 million park and event space would be built on the stadium's grounds, along with a mooring field in the waters of the Marine Stadium Basin and new marina facilities on Virginia Key.

Lawsuits were filed by the Village of Key Biscayne against the City of Miami seeking to stop the plans, claiming that the boat show and dozens of other events planned at the Miami Marine Stadium would lead to potentially dangerous congestion along the Rickenbacker Causeway. A separate lawsuit was filed against the NMMA, alleging that the NMMA had illegally negotiated its contract in private and denied the village's request for public records pertaining to land use, funding, profit sharing and correspondence between the boat show parent and the City of Miami.

Despite this, the City of Miami will continue with its plans, and the Miami International Boat Show plans to move onto the property by February 2016.

BIBLIOGRAPHY

Alen, Michael. "Chayo Frank: Architect for Amertec Building." Vimeo, 2014. https://vimeo.com/110371039.

Cagle, Mary. *NIKE AJAX Historical Monograph*. U.S. Army Ordnance Missile Command, 1959. http://www.historicbuckscounty.org/richboro/nike/nikeajax.pdf.

Eaton, Sarah E., and Ellen Eguccioni. *Coconut Grove Playhouse Designation Report*. Miami, FL: City of Miami Historic Preservation Board, 2005.

Estefan, Gloria. "An Open Letter to the City of Miami." City of Miami, 2014.

Frank, Chayo. "The Amertec Building." Chayo Frank, 2007. http://www.chayofrank.com/amertec-building.html.

Jacobs, James. *Historic American Buildings Survey, Monroe Station*. Washington, D.C.: National Park Service, 2007.

Larson, Eric. "Death in the Everglades." *TIME* (1996).

La Rue, Doug. *Aerojet-Dade: An Unfinished Journey*. Documentary. WKLG, 2009.

Melnick, Jordan. "The Death (and Life?) of Miami's Marine Stadium." Citylab, 2012. http://www.citylab.com/design/2012/03/miami-marine-stadium/1432.

Miranda, Carolina. "'Concrete Paradise,' an Exhibition on the Miami Marine Stadium, on View at Coral Gables Museum." *Architect Magazine* (2013). http://www.architectmagazine.com/design/culture/concrete-paradise-an-exhibition-on-the-miami-marine-stadium-on-view-at-coral-gables-museum_o.

Morgan, Richard. "Q&A: The Miami Marine Stadium's Architect on Its Past and Future." *Metropolis Magazine* (2015).

Morley, Jefferson. "Dirty Money." *Miami New Times*, 1991.

Posner, Gerald. *Miami Babylon*. New York: Simon & Schuster, 2009.

Richey, Warren. "U.S. Fights Spain's Refusal to Return Ex-Floridian to Face Charges." *Sun Sentinel*, 1995.

Smiley, David. "Gloria Estefan Hammers Marine Stadium Group after Failed Redevelopment Bid." *Miami Herald*, 2014

———. "Massive Miami Marine Stadium Plan Crumbles." *Miami Herald*, 2014.

Tester, Hank. "ValuJet Crash Remembered 15 Years Later." NBC Miami, 2011.

Willis, Eric. "An Architect and His Stadium." *Preservation Magazine* (2008).

INDEX

ABOUT THE AUTHOR

Born and raised in Miami, Florida, DAVID BULIT began urban exploring in 2009 after watching a documentary about the activity and becoming interested in the history people had left behind. His passion for photography grew from it as a way to share these places with others.

In 2010, he started his website "Abandoned Florida," which aims to document abandoned and forgotten places throughout the state of Florida, as well as promote and share the work of local artists, photographers and filmmakers with similar interests. You can visit it at www.abandonedfl.com.

CONTRIBUTING AUTHOR

JIM DOURNEY is an amateur historian, photographer, wanderer and avid outdoorsperson. A native Floridian with a passion for the history and flora and fauna of his home, he can be found wandering the back roads looking for points of interest. He logs his adventures at www.snookguy.com.

Visit us at
www.historypress.net

This title is also available as an e-book.

CPSIA information can be obtained
at www.ICGtesting.com
Printed in the USA
LVHW062334310820
664725LV00005B/53